VISION

GENERAL EDITORS

Dale C. Garell, M.D.
Medical Director, California Children Services, Department of Health
  Services, County of Los Angeles
Associate Dean for Curriculum
Clinical Professor, Department of Pediatrics & Family Medicine,
  University of Southern California School of Medicine
Former President, Society for Adolescent Medicine

Solomon H. Snyder, M.D.
Distinguished Service Professor of Neuroscience, Pharmacology, and
  Psychiatry, Johns Hopkins University School of Medicine
Former president, Society of Neuroscience
Albert Lasker Award in Medical Research, 1978

CONSULTING EDITORS

Robert W. Blum, M.D., Ph.D.
Associate Professor, School of Public Health and Department of
  Pediatrics
Director, Adolescent Health Program, University of Minnesota
Consultant, World Health Organization

Charles E. Irwin, Jr., M.D.
Associate Professor of Pediatrics; Director, Division of Adolescent
  Medicine, University of California, San Francisco

Lloyd J. Kolbe, Ph.D.
Chief, Office of School Health & Special Projects, Center for Health
  Promotion & Education, Centers for Disease Control
President, American School Health Association

Jordan J. Popkin
Director, Division of Federal Employee Occupational Health, U.S. Public
  Health Service Region I

Joseph L. Rauh, M.D.
Professor of Pediatrics and Medicine, Adolescent Medicine, Children's
  Hospital Medical Center, Cincinnati
Former president, Society for Adolescent Medicine

THE ENCYCLOPEDIA OF HEALTH

THE HEALTHY BODY

Dale C. Garell, M.D. · General Editor

VISION

Jane Samz

Introduction by C. Everett Koop, M.D., Sc.D.
former Surgeon General, U.S. Public Health Service

CHELSEA HOUSE PUBLISHERS
New York · Philadelphia

The goal of the ENCYCLOPEDIA OF HEALTH *is to provide general information in the ever-changing areas of physiology, psychology, and related medical issues. The titles in this series are not intended to take the place of the professional advice of a physician or other health care professional.*

Chelsea House Publishers
EDITOR-IN-CHIEF Nancy Toff
EXECUTIVE EDITOR Remmel T. Nunn
MANAGING EDITOR Karyn Gullen Browne
COPY CHIEF Juliann Barbato
PICTURE EDITOR Adrian G. Allen
ART DIRECTOR Maria Epes
MANUFACTURING MANAGER Gerald Levine

The Encyclopedia of Health
SENIOR EDITOR Paula Edelson

Staff for VISION
ASSISTANT EDITOR Laura Dolce
COPY EDITOR Michael Goodman
DEPUTY COPY CHIEF Mark Rifkin
EDITORIAL ASSISTANT Leigh Hope Wood
PICTURE RESEARCHER Sandy Jones and Bill Rice
ASSISTANT ART DIRECTOR Loraine Machlin
SENIOR DESIGNER Marjorie Zaum
DESIGN ASSISTANT Debora Smith
PRODUCTION MANAGER Joseph Romano
PRODUCTION COORDINATOR Marie Claire Cebrián

First Printing

1   3   5   7   9   8   6   4   2

Library of Congress Cataloging-in-Publication Data

Samz, Jane.
   Vision / Jane Samz.
      p.   cm.—(The Encyclopedia of health)
   Includes bibliographical references.
   Summary: Discusses the anatomy and common disorders of the eye.
   ISBN 0-7910-0031-1.
          0-7910-0471-6 (pbk.)
      1. Eye—Diseases and defects—Juvenile literature.   2. Vision disorders—Juvenile literature.   [1. Eye.   2. Vision disorders.]
I. Title.   II. Series.   89-71160
RE51.S193 1990   CIP
617.7—dc20   AC

CONTENTS

THE ENCYCLOPEDIA OF
H E A L T H

THE HEALTHY BODY

The Circulatory System
Dental Health
The Digestive System
The Endocrine System
Exercise
Genetics & Heredity
The Human Body: An Overview
Hygiene
The Immune System
Memory & Learning
The Musculoskeletal System
The Neurological System
Nutrition
The Reproductive System
The Respiratory System
The Senses
Speech & Hearing
Sports Medicine
Vision
Vitamins & Minerals

THE LIFE CYCLE

Adolescence
Adulthood
Aging
Childhood
Death & Dying
The Family
Friendship & Love
Pregnancy & Birth

MEDICAL ISSUES

Careers in Health Care
Environmental Health
Folk Medicine
Health Care Delivery
Holistic Medicine
Medical Ethics
Medical Fakes & Frauds
Medical Technology
Medicine & the Law
Occupational Health
Public Health

PSYCHOLOGICAL DISORDERS AND THEIR TREATMENT

Anxiety & Phobias
Child Abuse
Compulsive Behavior
Delinquency & Criminal Behavior
Depression
Diagnosing & Treating Mental Illness
Eating Habits & Disorders
Learning Disabilities
Mental Retardation
Personality Disorders
Schizophrenia
Stress Management
Suicide

MEDICAL DISORDERS AND THEIR TREATMENT

AIDS
Allergies
Alzheimer's Disease
Arthritis
Birth Defects
Cancer
The Common Cold
Diabetes
First Aid & Emergency Medicine
Gynecological Disorders
Headaches
The Hospital
Kidney Disorders
Medical Diagnosis
The Mind-Body Connection
Mononucleosis and Other Infectious Diseases
Nuclear Medicine
Organ Transplants
Pain
Physical Handicaps
Poisons & Toxins
Prescription & OTC Drugs
Sexually Transmitted Diseases
Skin Disorders
Stroke & Heart Disease
Substance Abuse
Tropical Medicine

PREVENTION AND EDUCATION: THE KEYS TO GOOD HEALTH

C. Everett Koop, M.D., Sc.D.

former Surgeon General,
U.S. Public Health Service

The issue of health education has received particular attention in recent years because of the presence of AIDS in the news. But our response to this particular tragedy points up a number of broader issues that doctors, public health officials, educators, and the public face. In particular, it points up the necessity for sound health education for citizens of all ages.

Over the past 25 years this country has been able to bring about dramatic declines in the death rates for heart disease, stroke, accidents, and, for people under the age of 45, cancer. Today, Americans generally eat better and take better care of themselves than ever before. Thus, with the help of modern science and technology, they have a better chance of surviving serious—even catastrophic—illnesses. That's the good news.

But, like every phonograph record, there's a flip side, and one with special significance for young adults. According to a report issued in 1979 by Dr. Julius Richmond, my predecessor as Surgeon General, Americans aged 15 to 24 had a higher death rate in 1979 than they did 20 years earlier. The causes: violent death and injury, alcohol and drug abuse, unwanted pregnancies, and sexually transmitted diseases. Adolescents are particularly vulnerable, because they are beginning to explore their own sexuality and perhaps to experiment with drugs. The need for educating young people is critical, and the price of neglect is high.

Yet even for the population as a whole, our health is still far from what it could be. Why? A 1974 Canadian government report attributed all death and disease to four broad elements: inadequacies in the health-care system, behavioral factors or unhealthy life-styles, environmental hazards, and human biological factors.

To be sure, there are diseases that are still beyond the control of even our advanced medical knowledge and techniques. And despite yearnings that are as old as the human race itself, there is no "fountain of youth" to ward off aging and death. Still, there is a solution to many of the problems that undermine sound health. In a word, that solution is prevention. Prevention, which includes health promotion and education, saves lives, improves the quality of life, and, in the long run, saves money.

In the United States, organized public health activities and preventive medicine have a long history. Important milestones include the improvement of sanitary procedures and the development of pasteurized milk in the late 19th century, and the introduction in the mid-20th century of effective vaccines against polio, measles, German measles, mumps, and other once-rampant diseases. Internationally, organized public health efforts began on a wide-scale basis with the International Sanitary Conference of 1851, to which 12 nations sent representatives. The World Health Organization, founded in 1948, continues these efforts under the aegis of the United Nations, with particular emphasis on combatting communicable diseases and the training of health-care workers.

But despite these accomplishments, much remains to be done in the field of prevention. For too long, we have had a medical care system that is science- and technology-based, focused, essentially, on illness and mortality. It is now patently obvious that both the social and the economic costs of such a system are becoming insupportable.

Implementing prevention—and its corollaries, health education and promotion—is the job of several groups of people:

First, the medical and scientific professions need to continue basic scientific research, and here we are making considerable progress. But increased concern with prevention will also have a decided impact on how primary-care doctors practice medicine. With a shift to health-based rather than morbidity-based medicine, the role of the "new physician" will include a healthy dose of patient education.

Second, practitioners of the social and behavioral sciences—psychologists, economists, city planners—along with lawyers, business leaders, and government officials—must solve the practical and ethical dilemmas confronting us: poverty, crime, civil rights, literacy, education, employment, housing, sanitation, environmental protection, health care delivery systems, and so forth. All of these issues affect public health.

Third is the public at large. We'll consider that very important group in a moment.

Fourth, and the linchpin in this effort, is the public health profession—doctors, epidemiologists, teachers—who must harness the professional expertise of the first two groups and the common sense and cooperation of the third, the public. They must define the problems statistically and qualitatively and then help us set priorities for finding the solutions.

To a very large extent, improving those statistics is the responsibility of every individual. So let's consider more specifically what the role of the individual should be and why health education is so important to that role. First, and most obviously, individuals can protect themselves from illness and injury and thus minimize their need for professional medical care. They can eat a nutritious diet, get adequate exercise, avoid tobacco, alcohol, and drugs, and take prudent steps to avoid accidents. The proverbial "apple a day keeps the doctor away" is not so far from the truth, after all.

Second, individuals should actively participate in their own medical care. They should schedule regular medical and dental checkups. Should they develop an illness or injury, they should know when to treat themselves and when to seek professional help. To gain the maximum benefit from any medical treatment that they do require, individuals must become partners in that treatment. For instance, they should understand the effects and side effects of medications. I counsel young physicians that there is no such thing as too much information when talking with patients. But the corollary is the patient must know enough about the nuts and bolts of the healing process to understand what the doctor is telling him. That is at least partially the patient's responsibility.

Education is equally necessary for us to understand the ethical and public policy issues in health care today. Sometimes individuals will encounter these issues in making decisions about their own treatment or that of family members. Other citizens may encounter them as jurors in medical malpractice cases. But we all become involved, indirectly, when we elect our public officials, from school board members to the president. Should surrogate parenting be legal? To what extent is drug testing desirable, legal, or necessary? Should there be public funding for family planning, hospitals, various types of medical research, and medical care for the indigent? How should we allocate scant technological resources, such as kidney dialysis and organ transplants? What is the proper role of government in protecting the rights of patients?

What are the broad goals of public health in the United States today? In 1980, the Public Health Service issued a report aptly en-

9

titled *Promoting Health-Preventing Disease: Objectives for the Nation.* This report expressed its goals in terms of mortality and in terms of intermediate goals in education and health improvement. It identified 15 major concerns: controlling high blood pressure; improving family planning; improving pregnancy care and infant health; increasing the rate of immunization; controlling sexually transmitted diseases; controlling the presence of toxic agents and radiation in the environment; improving occupational safety and health; preventing accidents; promoting water fluoridation and dental health; controlling infectious diseases; decreasing smoking; decreasing alcohol and drug abuse; improving nutrition; promoting physical fitness and exercise; and controlling stress and violent behavior.

For healthy adolescents and young adults (ages 15 to 24), the specific goal was a 20% reduction in deaths, with a special focus on motor vehicle injuries and alcohol and drug abuse. For adults (ages 25 to 64), the aim was 25% fewer deaths, with a concentration on heart attacks, strokes, and cancers.

Smoking is perhaps the best example of how individual behavior can have a direct impact on health. Today cigarette smoking is recognized as the most important single preventable cause of death in our society. It is responsible for more cancers and more cancer deaths than any other known agent; is a prime risk factor for heart and blood vessel disease, chronic bronchitis, and emphysema; and is a frequent cause of complications in pregnancies and of babies born prematurely, underweight, or with potentially fatal respiratory and cardiovascular problems.

Since the release of the Surgeon General's first report on smoking in 1964, the proportion of adult smokers has declined substantially, from 43% in 1965 to 30.5% in 1985. Since 1965, 37 million people have quit smoking. Although there is still much work to be done if we are to become a "smoke-free society," it is heartening to note that public health and public education efforts—such as warnings on cigarette packages and bans on broadcast advertising—have already had significant effects.

In 1835, Alexis de Tocqueville, a French visitor to America, wrote, "In America the passion for physical well-being is general." Today, as then, health and fitness are front-page items. But with the greater scientific and technological resources now available to us, we are in a far stronger position to make good health care available to everyone. And with the greater technological threats to us as we approach the 21st century, the need to do so is more urgent than ever before. Comprehensive information about basic biology, preventive medicine, medical and surgical treatments, and related ethical and public policy issues can help you arm yourself with the knowledge you need to be healthy throughout your life.

FOREWORD

Dale C. Garell, M.D.

Advances in our understanding of health and disease during the 20th century have been truly remarkable. Indeed, it could be argued that modern health care is one of the greatest accomplishments in all of human history. In the early 1900s, improvements in sanitation, water treatment, and sewage disposal reduced death rates and increased longevity. Previously untreatable illnesses can now be managed with antibiotics, immunizations, and modern surgical techniques. Discoveries in the fields of immunology, genetic diagnosis, and organ transplantation are revolutionizing the prevention and treatment of disease. Modern medicine is even making inroads against cancer and heart disease, two of the leading causes of death in the United States.

Although there is much to be proud of, medicine continues to face enormous challenges. Science has vanquished diseases such as smallpox and polio, but new killers, most notably AIDS, confront us. Moreover, we now victimize ourselves with what some have called "diseases of choice," or those brought on by drug and alcohol abuse, bad eating habits, and mismanagement of the stresses and strains of contemporary life. The very technology that is doing so much to prolong life has brought with it previously unimaginable ethical dilemmas related to issues of death and dying. The rising cost of health-care is a matter of central concern to us all. And violence in the form of automobile accidents, homicide, and suicide remain the major killers of young adults.

In the past, most people were content to leave health care and medical treatment in the hands of professionals. But since the 1960s, the consumer of medical care—that is, the patient—has assumed an increasingly central role in the management of his or her own health. There has also been a new emphasis placed on prevention: People are recognizing that their own actions can help prevent many of the conditions that have caused death and disease in the past. This accounts for the growing commitment to good nutrition and regular exercise, for the fact that more and more people are choosing not to smoke, and for a new moderation in people's drinking habits.

People want to know more about themselves and their own health. They are curious about their body: its anatomy, physiology, and biochemistry. They want to keep up with rapidly evolving medical technologies and procedures. They are willing to educate themselves about common disorders and diseases so that they can be full partners in their own health-care.

The ENCYCLOPEDIA OF HEALTH is designed to provide the basic knowledge that readers will need if they are to take significant responsibility for their own health. It is also meant to serve as a frame of reference for further study and exploration. The ENCYCLOPEDIA is divided into five subsections: The Healthy Body; The Life Cycle; Medical Disorders & Their Treatment; Psychological Disorders & Their Treatment; and Medical Issues. For each topic covered by the ENCYCLOPEDIA, we present the essential facts about the relevant biology; the symptoms, diagnosis, and treatment of common diseases and disorders; and ways in which you can prevent or reduce the severity of health problems when that is possible. The ENCYCLOPEDIA also projects what may lie ahead in the way of future treatment or prevention strategies.

The broad range of topics and issues covered in the ENCYCLOPEDIA reflects the fact that human health encompasses physical, psychological, social, environmental, and spiritual well-being. Just as the mind and the body are inextricably linked, so, too, is the individual an integral part of the wider world that comprises his or her family, society, and environment. To discuss health in its broadest aspect it is necessary to explore the many ways in which it is connected to such fields as law, social science, public policy, economics, and even religion. And so, the ENCYCLOPEDIA is meant to be a bridge between science, medical technology, the world at large, and you. I hope that it will inspire you to pursue in greater depth particular areas of interest, and that you will take advantage of the suggestions for further reading and the lists of resources and organizations that can provide additional information.

CHAPTER 1
THE EYE THROUGHOUT HISTORY

Egyptians from about A.D. 1000 study the way light reflects off water and affects the workings of the eye.

The human eye has been the subject of wonder and study for centuries. The ancient Egyptians were among the first to record their observations of the eye and eye disorders. Records of their findings, which may date back as far as 6,000 years, have been found in the ancient medical writings known as the Ebers Papyrus. Historians believe that eye surgery may actually have been performed more than 4,000 years ago. In support of this theory, they cite laws in the Code of Hammurabi dating back to

2100 B.C. that govern how any physician attempting to save a person's eye should be treated. According to the code, doctors were to be rewarded if the eye was saved and punished if the eye was lost. Other ancient medical treatments for eye diseases included acupuncture (a technique first used by the Chinese at least 2,000 years ago that involves inserting needles at special points throughout the body to relieve pain) and an operation to remove cataracts practiced in India and the Mediterranean area about 2,400 to 3,000 years ago.

Although the ancients obviously discovered some facts about the eye and made efforts to treat its diseases, many earlier civilizations did not have a full understanding of the organ or of its functions. In fact, although physicians performed operations to remove cataracts, they did not fully understand that a cataract is a milky-white film covering the lens of the eye. The first to ascertain more about the organ was the Greek scientist Alcmaeon, who, in about 600 B.C., dissected a human eye. During his dissection, Alcmaeon discovered paths linking the eye to the brain. These paths, he believed, carried light, and therefore the images people see, to the brain. Today scientists know that Alcmaeon's paths were in fact nerves.

In the early 1600s, the German astronomer-mathematician Johannes Kepler theorized that humans see an object because its image is formed on the retina. A few years later, the French

The German astronomer Johannes Kepler was the first to theorize that sight results from the projection of an image onto the retina.

From his studies of the eye of an ox, René Descartes determined that the image that forms on the retina is upside down.

philosopher-mathematician René Descartes, in studying the eye of an ox, found that Kepler was right. Images of objects did form on the retina. But, Descartes discovered, those images were not formed as people actually see them. The images on the retina were not right side up, they were upside down.

In 1668, the eye's blind spot was discovered by the French scientist Edme Mariotte. This blind spot, scientists now know, is the place where the optic nerve meets the retina.

FURTHER DISCOVERIES

In 1801, English physicist Thomas Young hypothesized that the eye responded to three colors of light—red, green, and violet. In the mid-1800s, the German physicist Hermann von Helmholtz developed this theory further. Today scientists know that the eye has special "color receptors," known as cones, that respond to red, green, and blue light. The theory is known as the Young-Helmholtz trichromatic (three-color) theory.

In 1851, Helmholtz invented the ophthalmoscope, which allowed an observer to shine a beam of light into the eye and observe the eye's lighted interior with the aid of a series of lenses. One of the first uses of the ophthalmoscope was to examine eyes damaged by sunlight. The ophthalmoscope was also used to study the eyes of victims of a strange eye disorder who were found to have pigment forming on their retinas. (Today this disease is known as retinitis pigmentosa [RP], which will be further discussed in Chapter 7.)

In 1835, British surgeon Dr. S. L. Bigger performed the first successful corneal transplant—surgically replacing a diseased or damaged cornea with a new one—on an animal. And, in 1905, the first successful human corneal transplant was performed by the Czechoslovakian doctor Eduard Zirm.

In 1920, the Swiss ophthalmologist Dr. Jules Gonin discovered that it was not inevitable that victims of detached retina lose their sight, as had been believed in the past. Instead, Gonin found that the retina could be put back in place and repaired.

In the 1940s, British ophthalmologist Harold Ridley attempted the first intraocular lens implant, replacing a cataract victim's own clouded lens with a plastic lens. Ridley had first conceived of the idea of using a plastic lens during World War II while treating wounded airmen for eye injuries. When fighter planes' plastic windows shattered, pieces of plastic sometimes flew into the eyes of some of the airmen. Yet the plastic itself did not seem

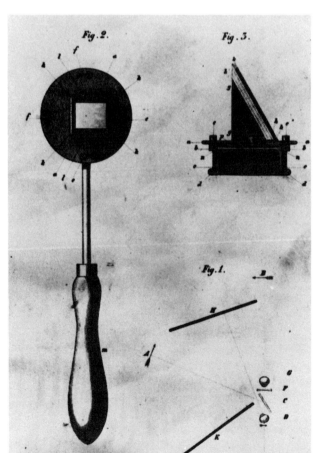

Hermann von Helmholtz's ophthalmoscope (Figure 2) and assorted medical instruments. The invention of the ophthalmoscope paved the way for greater precision in the identification of eye disorders.

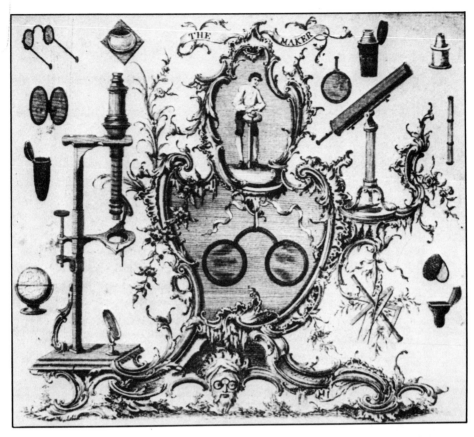

An optician's business card depicts the process of spectacle making in 1750.

to harm their eyes. However, it was not until the 1960s that intraocular implants became truly successful.

A BRIEF HISTORY OF LENSES

The history of using glass for correcting vision begins with the ancient Romans, who discovered that writing appeared clearer and larger when seen through a crystal bowl filled with water. (The water-filled bowl acted like a magnifying glass.)

In the 13th century, magnifying glasses were in use as reading glasses in both Europe and China; lenses for nearsighted people were developed later—in the 16th century. Also in the 16th century, the great Renaissance scientist-inventor-artist Leonardo da Vinci developed a design for contact lenses. Unfortunately, Leonardo's design remained on paper and was not to be developed until nearly 300 years later.

During the 1700s, American scientist-statesman Benjamin Franklin invented the first bifocals, and in 1887 Swiss doctor A. Eugen Fick made the first contact lenses, out of glass. The first plastic contact lenses, made of hard plastic, were invented in 1938. In 1958, the first bifocal contact lenses were introduced. And the first soft contact lenses were developed in 1970.

Today there are not only regular hard and soft contact lenses but also new gas-permeable hard lenses, which enable the cornea to receive more oxygen than regular hard lenses allow; extended-wear soft contact lenses, made of very thin soft plastic; contact lenses—both hard and soft—for people with astigmatism (a visual defect caused by curvature of the cornea or lens); lenses to change the wearer's eye color; and even disposable contacts to wear for a few days' time, then throw away.

It is likely that almost everyone uses at least one of these eye inventions or knows someone who does. To understand the purpose behind such devices more fully, it is first necessary to explore the organ for which they are intended—the eye.

•   •   •   •

CHAPTER 2

THE ANATOMY
OF THE EYE

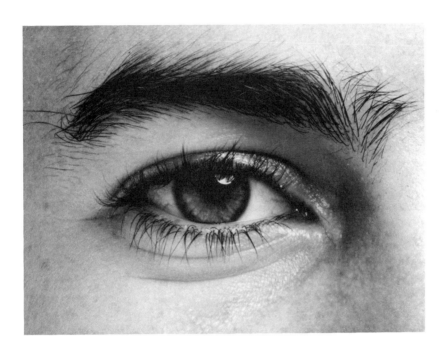

Although the human eye is actually quite delicate, it is protected from harm by the bones that surround it and by the eyebrows, eyelids, eyelashes, and tear glands. The eye rests in, and is shielded by, a bony socketlike area in the head known as the orbit. A layer of fat helps cushion the eye from impact. Six muscles outside the eyeball itself (the extraocular muscles) enable the eye to move from side to side and up and down. The eyebrows, eyelids, and eyelashes help prevent dust and other

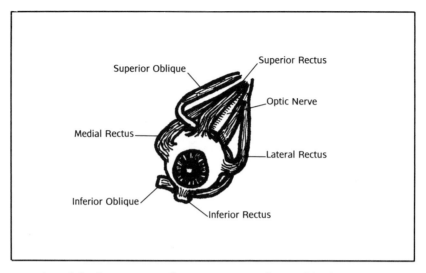

Muscles of the human eye. These seven muscles enable the eye to move up and down and from side to side.

foreign objects from invading the eye. In addition, the eyelids (made up in part by the thinnest skin found on the human body) help distribute tears from the lachrymal (tear) glands over the surface of the eye. The tears not only keep the eye moist; they also help wash away dust and foreign objects that the eyebrows, eyelids, and eyelashes alone are unable to keep out of the eye.

The eye itself consists of the conjunctiva, sclera and cornea, iris and pupil, lens, vitreous humor, aqueous humor, choroid, and retina. The conjunctiva, the innermost layer of the eyelid, is a thin, transparent membrane that covers the sclera—visible as the white of the eye. The conjunctiva helps lubricate the eye by producing mucus and some tears. It is extremely sensitive to stimuli. Its sensitivity enables the eye to react very quickly to any foreign object that comes in contact with the conjunctiva and thus protects it from injury. The lachrymal glands are also stimulated by alien objects, producing tears that frequently wash them out of the eye. Something as small as an eyelash will produce an uncomfortable sensation and cause the eye to tear and become red and irritated.

The most sensitive region of the eye is the cornea. Even a very tiny scratch on the cornea can be extremely painful and should be treated at once by an eye doctor. For if the cornea is damaged, scar tissue may form a leukoma—an opaque spot that may interfere with vision.

The cornea covers the iris, the colored part of the eye. The iris's color comes from melanin, the same pigment that gives color to the skin when exposed to sunlight. People with blue eyes have a small amount of melanin in their iris, whereas people with larger amounts of melanin may have green, hazel, gray, or brown eyes. The amount of melanin found in a person's iris and the color of that person's eyes are a matter of genetics. In addition to giving the iris its color, melanin helps protect the eye from excessive light. Albinos—people with little or no melanin in their skin, hair, and eyes—are usually extremely sensitive to light.

The small black spot at the center of the iris is the pupil. It is really an opening in the iris that looks black because it does not reflect light. This opening grows smaller or larger to control how much light enters the eye. Muscles in the iris control the pupil's size, causing it to expand in dim light and contract in bright light.

A horizontal section of the eyeball. Light must pass through the cornea, aqueous humor, pupil, lens, and vitreous humor to reach the retina.

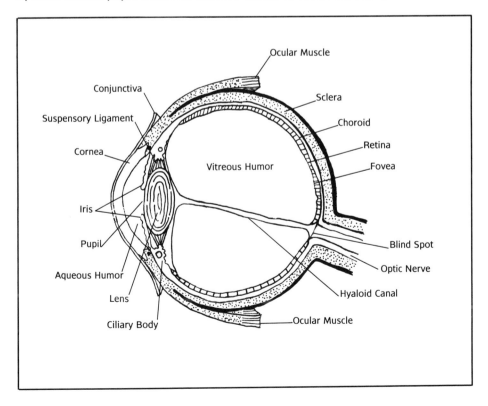

During an examination, an eye doctor may dim the lights in the room and observe the pupil as it expands and contracts by shining a small penlight at it. In addition, some eye doctors give their patients special eye drops that force the pupil to expand, thus allowing the doctor to more fully examine the eye.

The pupil and the iris, together with the choroid, make up the part of the eye known as the uveal tract. The uveal tract is a pigmented middle layer that lies between the sclera and the retina. Although the iris and pupil are both located at the anterior portion of the eye, the choroid makes up the posterior section and contains most of the blood vessels that nourish the eye.

Behind the iris lies the lens of the eye. The lens is held in place by ligaments known as the zonules of Zinn, which are attached to the ciliary body. (The ciliary body is a muscular body that makes up the third portion of the uveal tract.) The lens of the eye, together with the cornea, acts to focus the light rays on the retina, permitting transmission of the image to the brain. Since the cornea's shape is normally fixed, the only way that a person's eyes can focus clearly on both near and distant objects is for the lens itself to change shape. This transformation is accomplished with the help of the ciliary muscle. When someone looks at distant objects, the ciliary muscle relaxes. This relaxation pulls on the zonules, which then pull on, and flatten, the lens. The ciliary muscle contracts when the subject views an object nearby. As the ciliary muscle contracts, the zonules loosen, and the lens thickens and becomes more curved. In this way, the thinner, flatter lens brings light rays from distant objects into focus; the thicker, more curved lens is able to focus light rays from nearby objects.

Between the cornea and the front surface of the lens is the space called the anterior chamber. Between the back of the iris and the lens lies the posterior chamber. A clear fluid, the aqueous humor, flows through the posterior and anterior chambers, leaving the eye through Schlemm's canal. Normally, the amount of aqueous humor produced by the ciliary body is balanced by the amount of aqueous humor that leaves the eye through this canal. Sometimes the system becomes unbalanced, however, and fluid pressure builds up, resulting in a dangerous condition known as glaucoma. (For more on glaucoma, see Chapter 6.) Behind the lens lies the vitreous body. Instead of a thin, watery fluid like aqueous humor, the vitreous body is filled with a thick, jellylike substance known as vitreous humor.

Near the back of the eye lies the retina, an extremely thin, delicate layer that acts somewhat like the film in a camera. The retina collects the light that has entered the eye through the pupil and has been focused by the lens. From there, nerve cells in the retina begin the process of sending that image on to the brain, where real "seeing" actually takes place. The images that are focused on the retina are actually inverted—what scientists call real images. (They are upside down and reversed from left to right.) These images—in the form of electrical impulses—are sent, via the optic nerve, to the brain, where they are essentially turned right side up again. The point at which the optic nerve meets the retina is known as the blind spot. This is because there are no light-sensitive cells at this point in the retina.

Rods and cones. Rods provide humans with black-and-white vision; cones enable the eye to perceive color.

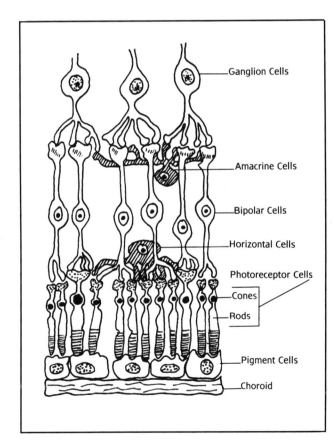

The retina has two kinds of light-sensitive nerve cells, called rods and cones. The rods, which are located mostly on the sides of the retina, provide humans with black-and-white vision and allow them to see in dim light. This is why, when someone sees a faint star out of the corner of his or her eye and turns to look at it, it seems to disappear. The cones are found mainly in the central region of the retina, which is known as the macula (or macula lutea). The cones are responsible for color vision. Since the cones work best in bright light, it becomes difficult to see colors outdoors at night or in a darkened room. The regions of the retina outside the macula are responsible for peripheral (side) vision. The area of sharpest vision, however, is at the fovea centralis in the center of the macula. This is why, given enough light to activate the cones, people see things best when they look straight at them.

ACCOMMODATION

Under normal circumstances, the lens of the eye changes shape to accommodate a shift in focus—from looking at objects close up to viewing them at a distance. This would accommodate a change from reading a book, for example, to looking out a window. In young people, the process of accommodation works quite well—and for great changes in distance—unless they are quite nearsighted or farsighted to begin with. Newborns and small infants generally can focus on objects located three inches or less from their eyes. Teenagers usually can focus on objects closer than about four inches from their eyes. With age, however, the lens of the eye becomes less and less elastic, and the ciliary muscle cannot change the shape of a more rigid lens as well as it could a more elastic one. Thus, with increasing age many people will need reading glasses in order to focus on objects held at arm's length from their eyes.

DEPTH PERCEPTION

If everyone had the use of only one eye, the world would look quite different. Everything would appear flat, and it would be hard to judge how far away objects really are. Without binocular

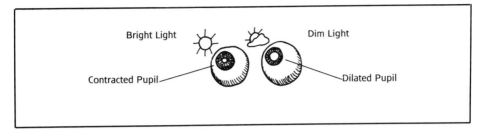

Muscles in the iris dilate or constrict the pupil to regulate the amount of light entering the eye.

vision (the view of the world seen through two eyes), humans would have no depth perception. Because people's eyes are set a certain distance apart in their head, each eye gets a slightly different view of the same scene. If a person covers one eye and looks around, then switches eyes and looks around again, the view will not be exactly the same. Certain objects, in fact, will not be seen at all or will be seen from a very different angle. But when those two slightly different images reach the brain at the same time, the brain combines them to form a single image that has depth to it. This is what is known as depth perception.

DARK AND LIGHT ADAPTATION

If a person walks from a lighted lobby into the theater just as the movie is starting, it may take several seconds, or even several minutes, for his or her eyes to adjust to the dark before being able to discern an empty seat. When the movie is over and the same person leaves the theater and returns to a sunny street, he or she may feel some pain by the sudden flooding of light and may have to squint for a while in order to see correctly. After a short time, however, that person's eyes will adjust to the new light. Of course, such an adjustment is accomplished by the expansion or contraction of the pupils. But it takes more than just a change in the size of a person's pupils to allow his or her eyes to adjust to changes in surrounding light levels.

The retina also plays an important role in light and dark adaptation. It is the rods of the retina that allow people to see in dim light. This is accomplished because of a pigment in the rods—known as rhodopsin (or visual purple). If a person has become adjusted to the dark and suddenly a bright light shines in his or her face, it will take a few minutes—perhaps even a half hour or more—to become fully adapted to darkness again. This is because bright lights bleach out the rhodopsin in the rods; it will take a certain amount of time for the rhodopsin in the rods to be restored so that the person can see in the dark once again. For this reason, astronomers, who are constantly switching from observing the night sky to reading a chart, use flashlights covered with red cellophane. Because the red light does not affect the eyes as much as the uncovered flashlight would, after the chart has been read, the eyes can switch their focus immediately back to the sky. Although it may take a while for night sight to return to a person once he or she has been exposed to bright light, the reverse of this is not quite the same. Adapting to bright lights after being in the dark is a much faster process—taking much less time—and is accomplished by both the cones and nerve cells in the retina.

The workings of the human eye are amazingly intricate and complex. Furthermore, they are all accomplished without requiring the conscious desire to see a particular object. For this reason, most people take their sight for granted, only giving it thought when it begins to give them trouble. But like any other part of the human body, the eye needs care and attention. And just as most people have their bodies examined during a yearly physical, the eyes deserve an annual examination as well.

●   ●   ●   ●

AN EYE EXAM

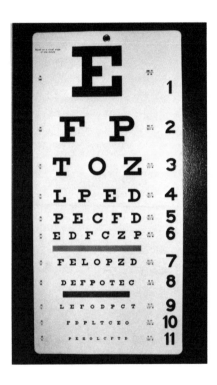

Tony was the star of the school's baseball team. He could spot a fly ball hit to the outfield long before anyone else. He was also fun to have on car trips, for he made a game of reading just part of a billboard and asking his friends to guess what the rest of it said before they could actually read it. But Tony had a hard time when it came to reading books. Because his eyes tired easily, he could read only for short periods of time. After discussing his

27

problem with his parents, Tony decided to visit an ophthalmologist to see what was wrong.

VISUAL HEALTH CARE PROFESSIONALS

Ophthalmologists are medical doctors who specialize in examining and treating eyes. After graduating from college, prospective ophthalmologists attend medical school to obtain their medical degrees—usually a four-year process. They then spend five years in special training in a hospital, first as interns, then as residents. As interns, they learn the same things any doctor in training learns: how to treat illnesses and how to respond to medical emergencies. As residents they start putting what they had learned as interns into practice, under the close supervision of a staff physician. After completing their residency, they spe-

A customer at a spectacle maker's shop in Frankfurt, Germany, 1568. Glasses were once thought to cause an evil distortion of nature, but their obvious usefulness soon overcame any objections.

cialize in ophthalmology. Ophthalmologists, sometimes called oculists, can not only examine a person's eyes and prescribe eyeglasses or contact lenses; they can also prescribe medication. For example, a person's eyes might become red and itchy during hayfever season. An ophthalmologist can prescribe allergy pills or eye drops that contain allergy medicine to help eliminate the redness and irritation. Ophthalmologists also prescribe medication to clear up eye infections and to treat diseases such as glaucoma. Some ophthalmologists, known as ophthalmologic surgeons, specialize in operating on people's eyes to try to prevent blindness.

Not everyone who visits an eye doctor, however, sees an ophthalmologist. Eye specialists who do not have M.D. degrees are known as optometrists. Optometrists can also examine eyes and prescribe glasses or contact lenses; in fact, optometrists will even fit a person with those glasses or contacts. Ophthalmologists will usually send the patient to an optician—a person who will make, and fit the patient with, the eyeglasses or contact lenses that ophthalmologists prescribe. But although optometrists are doctors, they are doctors of optometry, not medical doctors. They cannot prescribe medication, and they cannot perform eye surgery.

The training of optometrists is a bit different from that of ophthalmologists. After graduating from college, students of optometry attend a four-year school (or college) to earn their O.D. (doctor of optometry) degree. Then they must take and pass a test in order to be licensed to practice optometry. Although they cannot treat medical problems, optometrists have been trained to detect them. In this way they are able to refer those patients who do have medical eye problems to an ophthalmologist.

THE EYE EXAM

Before beginning an eye exam, both ophthalmologists and optometrists need to obtain a medical history. It may entail asking whether the patient has had such childhood diseases as measles, rubella (German measles), chicken pox, or scarlet fever, for these diseases can affect one's vision. The examiner may also ask whether the patient or other members of his or her family have, or have had, certain diseases or medical conditions, such as high blood pressure, diabetes, or glaucoma. The doctor will question the patient as to the present condition of his or her eyes: Are they itchy? Does the patient rub them a lot? Are they ever red or swollen? Is there any blurred vision? Any headaches? Does the patient suffer from any allergies? Does he or she have trouble seeing things close up or far away? Do the eyes tire easily?

After listening to the answers to these questions, the doctor will check the patient's vision by asking him or her to read an eye chart with one eye covered, then the other. The top line of an eye chart has one large letter; the second line has two smaller letters; the third line has several even smaller letters. And, with each line below that, the letters get still smaller and smaller. As the patient reads the chart, first with one eye, then the other, then with both eyes, the doctor can determine how good the subject's distance vision is. (For very young children, doctors may use an eye chart consisting of just a number of letter E's facing in all different directions rather than the chart adults use. In this

Eye charts are used to determine whether a person has normal vision or suffers from some visual disorder, such as nearsightedness or farsightedness.

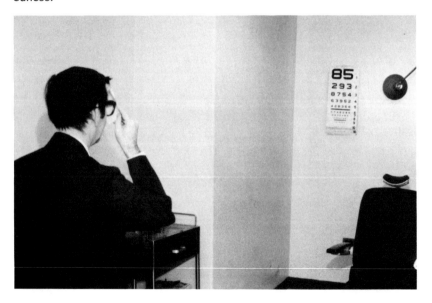

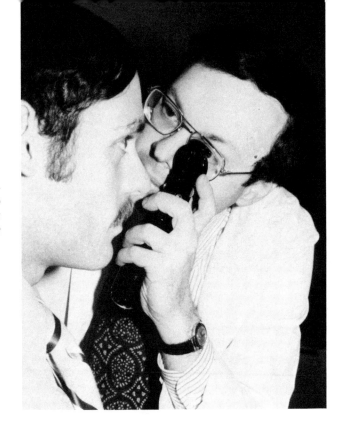

An ophthalmoscope enables the eye doctor to determine what eyeglass prescription, if any, the patient may need.

way children who may not yet know the alphabet can still be tested with accuracy. Children are simply asked to tell the doctor in which direction the **E** is pointing.)

If a patient is 20 feet from the eye chart and can read a line of letters that a person with normal vision can read from 20 feet away, that patient's vision is said to be 20/20. If that patient can read, at a distance of 20 feet, the line a person with normal vision can read from 15 feet away, that patient's vision is 20/15, and he or she is farsighted. (The patient can see things that are far away but has trouble seeing things that are close up.) If, however, the patient is 20 feet from the eye chart and can just make out the line of letters that a person with normal vision can read from 50 feet away, his or her vision is 20/50. This means that the patient is nearsighted; he or she can see and read things that are close up but may have trouble seeing things that are far away.

After the chart test is completed, the doctor may ask the patient to read a page of a book with lines of type that grow gradually

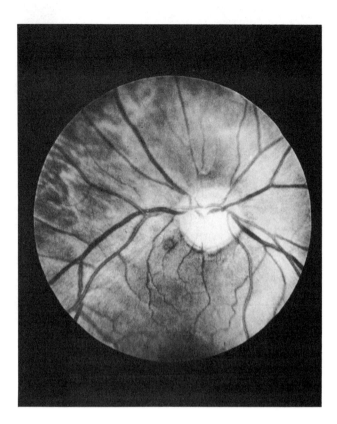

The inside of the eye as seen through an ophthalmoscope.

smaller. This test gives the eye doctor an idea of how good the patient's near vision is.

After testing the patient's vision, the doctor will usually examine the eyes. The patient is asked to stare straight ahead while the doctor examines his or her eyes with an ophthalmoscope. The ophthalmoscope has a small battery-operated light that the doctor shines into the patient's eyes. In addition, it has a series of lenses that enables the doctor to focus the light inside the patient's eye. With this instrument, the doctor can see whether or not the inside of the patient's eye looks normal. From this examination, the doctor can also make a fairly accurate estimate of what eyeglass prescription, if any, the patient will need.

If glasses are needed, the doctor will try a series of different lenses on the patient. The patient responds by telling the doctor which lens or lenses most improve his or her vision. In order to judge this, the patient will look at the eye chart with one eye while wearing a lens and continue this process until lenses are chosen for both eyes. This may be accomplished by wearing a special set of glasses that holds many different lenses or by looking into a machine equipped with many different lenses.

ADDITIONAL TESTS

Once the lenses have been chosen, the doctor may ask the patient to wear them and look once again at the letters on the eye chart. While the patient is doing this, the doctor will shine green and red lights on the chart and ask the patient if the letters look darker

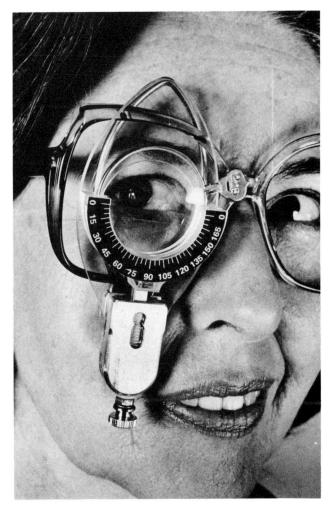

This device helps determine the most comfortable vertical position for bifocal lenses.

against a green background than they do against a red one, or vice versa. The doctor will then adjust the lenses accordingly. The doctor will check each eye separately, then both eyes at the same time. Ideally, the letters should appear equally dark on both backgrounds. Sometimes, however, what works well for each eye individually does not work as well when the patient uses both eyes at once. In this case, the doctor will once again adjust the lenses (until the patient sees things clearly). After the correct prescription has been determined and the patient is wearing the tester lenses, the doctor will shine a light once again into both eyes to determine to what extent the patient's vision has improved with the corrective lenses.

Once this has been accomplished, the doctor may wish to test the patient's visual field. He does so by darkening the room and flashing light on different parts of the wall in front of the patient. The patient is then asked to push a button each time he or she sees a flash of light. The button is attached to a machine that records the position of the light at the time the patient pushes the button and gives the doctor a printout of the patient's visual field.

Once the doctor has tested the visual field, he or she may wish to test the patient's color vision. The patient is asked to identify shapes made of multicolored dots set against a background of dots of other colors. The tests will enable the doctor to judge whether the patient is color-blind. In one case, there may be green dots making up an *X* surrounded by other dots of gray. A person who cannot see greens would not see that *X*. To him (most people suffering from color blindness are men), the dots that make up the *X* would look just as gray as the surrounding dots. For a further explanation of color blindness, please see p. 46. Before the exam is considered complete, the doctor should check the pressure inside each eye to test for glaucoma. Although young people rarely need to be tested for glaucoma, adults should have the test done every year or two. The doctor may put drops in the patient's eyes to numb the corneas and then press in on them with an instrument called a tonometer. (Some types of tonometers use a puff of air to press against the corneas and can be used without eye drops.) The tonometer measures how much pressure the eyeball exerts outward as the tonometer presses

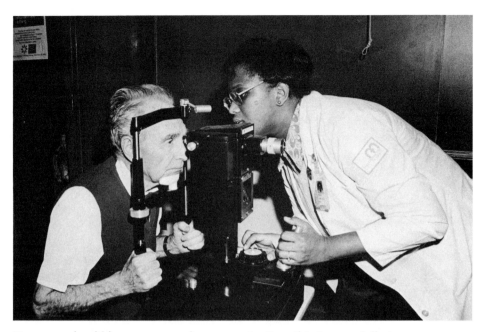

Everyone should have an annual eye examination; this is especially true for the elderly, whose eye muscles tend to become rigid, causing far-sightedness.

inward. The doctor needs to know if the pressure in a patient's eyes is too high before adding any drops that might make the pressure rise even more. If the pressure inside a person's eyes is too high, he or she has glaucoma. If the disease is left untreated, the pressure can damage the retina, and the person will slowly lose sight in the affected eye or eyes.

If the tonometer test is normal, the doctor may want to put other drops in the patient's eyes. The eye drops cause the pupils of the eyes to dilate (grow larger). They also prevent the pupils from contracting (getting smaller) when the doctor shines a light in them. The patient may be asked to sit in the waiting room for a while, because these drops take a few minutes to work. Because the drops dilate the pupils, they make it easier for the doctor to get a really good look at the eyes' internal structures. But because the drops prevent the pupils from constricting, the patient's vision—especially close up—may be blurry for a few hours afterward.

In most cases, the eye exam is complete after all of the above tests. Some doctors may not even use all of them in a routine exam. In any case, annual eye examinations are important not only to determine whether a person is nearsighted or farsighted but also to detect and treat one of the diseases that may strike the eye. These conditions—from simple nearsightedness to severe glaucoma—are the subject of the next few chapters.

• • • •

COMMON VISUAL DISORDERS

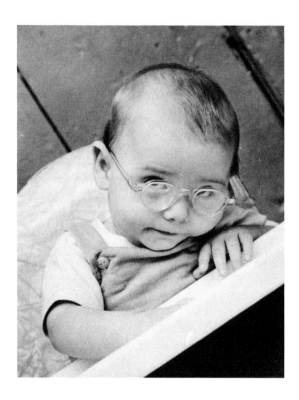

Millions of people throughout the world suffer from visual problems. Many of the conditions were probably discovered when they first started school. Perhaps they could not see the blackboard from the last row of seats in class, or they suffered from headaches while doing their homework. Whatever the case, visual problems are not at all uncommon and can crop up at any time in a person's life. A discussion of some of the more typical and easily treated visual disorders follows.

How the world looks to a nearsighted person. Also called myopia, near-sightedness occurs when the eyeball is longer (front to back) than normal.

NEARSIGHTEDNESS

In a nearsighted eye, light rays from nearby objects focus on the retina, but light rays from distant objects focus in front of the retina. So, although nearby objects are sharply in focus, distant objects look blurred.

Nearsightedness, also known as myopia, generally occurs because the eyeball is longer than normal; thus, light rays must travel farther than they would in a normal-size eye in order to reach the retina. Consequently, the light rays are more likely to focus in front of the retina. But nearsightedness can also occur in a normal-size eye if the cornea is more sharply curved than normal or if the lens of the eye is more sharply curved than that of a normal eye. But whether the eyeball is too long or the cornea or lens is too highly curved, doctors believe that the myopic eye's refractive power (its power to "bend" light rays)—also called its dioptric power—is too great.

Although scientists believe that the disorder may be inherited, babies are not usually born nearsighted. Generally, myopia first strikes when a child is about five to eight years old. It usually gets worse for a few years, although it may also remain stable for a short period. However, when the myopic youngster becomes a teenager and goes through a period of rapid growth, his or her myopia often worsens. Fortunately for most people suffering from nearsightedness, their disorder usually will not worsen much once they reach their twenties.

To correct myopia, eye doctors prescribe eyeglasses or contact lenses with concave lenses (lenses that are thin in the middle and thicker at the edges) to help focus distant light rays on, rather than in front of, the retina. Contact lenses for myopic eyes may be hard or soft contact lenses, or extended-wear lenses.

Hard contact lenses are tiny, rigid pieces of plastic about the size of the eye's iris—or smaller. These lenses usually just cover the tip of the little finger. Because they are so small, they are usually tinted so that they are easier to spot if they are dropped or fall out of the eye. Tinting also may help cut down a bit on glare, making the wearer more comfortable in bright lights, but such tinted contacts do not act like sunglasses. Hard lenses are

A depiction of farsighted vision. Farsightedness—or hyperopia—results when the eyeball is shorter than normal.

easy to "pop" into the eyes, but they can also pop out fairly easily—often by accident. Hard lenses float on a layer of tears and can shift around in the eye. And because hard lenses do not cling to the eye tightly, dust or eyelashes can get under the lenses. If this happens, the lenses must be removed and cleaned as soon as possible. Most hard lenses sold today are gas permeable: They are more comfortable than regular hard lenses because they allow more oxygen to reach the cornea.

Soft lenses are much thinner and larger than hard lenses, covering not only the iris but part of the sclera as well. Soft lenses are very flexible. In fact, it is possible—albeit uncomfortable— for wearers to wear them inside out. Because they are so thin and can tear so easily, soft lenses must be handled very carefully. Soft lenses absorb water and must remain wet in order to stay flexible. If they dry out, they become very brittle and can break easily. Moreover, because they absorb water, they must be sterilized—either by boiling or by using certain chemical solutions, such as a mild solution of hydrogen peroxide—before each wearing. Soft lenses cling more tightly to the eye than do hard lenses, so dust and eyelashes are less likely to get under them. Soft lenses are also much easier to get used to than hard lenses. Those who use hard contact lenses often break in their new lenses by wearing them for an hour longer each day; the entire process sometimes takes weeks. Many soft-contact wearers, by contrast, can wear their lenses for four hours or more on the first day. However, lens wearers should always follow the schedule their eye doctor recommends and not wait until their eyes bother them before taking their contacts out.

FARSIGHTEDNESS

Farsightedness could be said to be the opposite of nearsightedness. People who are farsighted, or have hyperopia, can see distant objects clearly but have trouble seeing objects that are close up.

Farsightedness generally occurs because there is less distance than normal between the cornea and the retina. A farsighted person's eyeballs are shorter than normal, so most light rays— especially those from nearby objects—reach the retina before

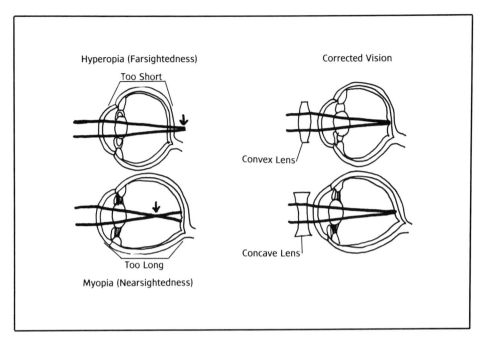

In hyperopia and myopia, light rays converge in front of or behind the retina. A convex lens will correct hyperopia, and a concave one repairs myopia.

they get a chance to come into focus. The result is a blurred image. Doctors say that the hyperopic eye has too little refractive power. In a number of cases of hyperopia, the eyeball is so short that even light rays from distant objects would reach the retina before they had a chance to focus—if it were not for the lens's ability to change shape and allow those distant light rays to focus on the retina after all.

The lens of a normal eye is fairly flat when viewing distant objects. However, the lens becomes thicker automatically when the eye shifts to nearby objects. This thickening allows light rays from nearby objects to focus on the retina. The lens's ability to change shape so that the eye can continue to stay in focus as it shifts from distant to near objects—or vice versa— is called accommodation.

Unfortunately, the lens of a farsighted eye cannot accommodate enough to allow for clear close-up vision. And, in many cases, the eyeball is so short that the lens must accommodate even when viewing distant objects. This means that the eye muscles in a hyperopic eye are often working overtime, continuing to adjust the thickness of the lens. This can lead to both eyestrain and headaches.

To correct hyperopia, eye doctors prescribe eyeglasses or contact lenses with convex lenses (lenses that are thick in the middle and thinner at the edges) to help focus light rays from nearby objects on, rather than behind, the retina. Convex lenses are also known as magnifying lenses.

PRESBYOPIA

Unfortunately, as adults grow older, their eyes often lose the ability to accommodate for vision as well as they did when they were younger. This condition, which generally begins to affect individuals in their forties or fifties, is known as presbyopia. What occurs with presbyopia is that the lens of the eye hardens and becomes less flexible with age. Because of the deterioration in the elasticity of the lens, an individual loses the clear close-up vision he or she had in childhood.

When a child is very young, he or she can focus on objects that are very close to the eyes. At the age of 10, the average youngster can still focus on objects only 3 inches from the eyes. However, by the time he or she is 12, the closest point at which an object can be held and still be in focus—called the near point of accommodation—has already lengthened to about 4 inches from the eyes. This distance stretches to about 6 to 10 inches by the age of 40 and increases much further, to about 39 inches (1 meter) by the age of 60.

As the lenses of the eyes become increasingly rigid, making close work more and more blurry, there may also be frequent eyestrain and headaches. Because of this, most older people cannot read without glasses. Those who needed glasses in their younger days may now need two pairs: one for distance and one for reading. To avoid carrying an extra pair of eyeglasses, many people wear bifocals instead.

Bifocals allow a person to wear two different eyeglass prescriptions at once. The prescription for distance vision is in the top section of the glasses. The prescription for reading is in the lower section. Some people, such as artists, who do a lot of work at intermediate distances (about arm's length), suffer from presbyopia and need trifocals. The top section of the trifocal lenses, again, is for distance vision; the bottom is for reading. But now there is also a middle section, which contains the prescription for intermediate-distance vision. Both bifocals and trifocals take some getting used to. The wearer has to be careful to use the reading section (which acts like a magnifying glass) only when reading and not to look down through it when walking. It can be especially dangerous to peer through the bottom section of such glasses when stepping off a curb or walking up and down stairs, for example.

People with presbyopia who have trouble with bifocal eyeglasses or those who are already wearing contact lenses may prefer to wear bifocal contact lenses. Bifocal contacts are designed with a central circle that contains the correction for distance vision. Surrounding that circle is an outer ring that contains the prescription the patient needs for reading.

ASTIGMATISM

When vision is distorted at any distance and nearsightedness or farsightedness cannot be corrected with glasses, the problem is

This distortion is caused by an astigmatism, the result of an unevenly shaped cornea or lens.

astigmatism. Astigmatism occurs because of an irregularly shaped cornea or lens (or both). As light rays pass through an uneven curvature of the cornea or lens, some of them will scatter. So, although some of the light rays may focus on the retina, as they would in a nonastigmatic eye, some will focus in front of the retina, and some will focus behind.

Some people are born astigmatic. Others may develop astigmatism as a result of an eye injury or a disease that scars the cornea. Generally, astigmatism can be corrected with eyeglasses or contact lenses that have cylindrical lenses. Light rays that hit the eyes come from many different directions. What cylindrical lenses do is bend some of those light rays (rays that come from one particular direction) more than others. This allows most—if not all—of the light that enters the eye to focus on the retina so that vision is clearer.

Contact lenses often clear up astigmatism better than glasses can because the outside of the contact lens is smoothly shaped, making the light rays that enter the eye behave as though they were passing through a smooth, rather than a bumpy, cornea. Unfortunately, people who have severe corneal astigmatism may not be able to wear contacts comfortably. In some cases, a hard lens specially designed to fit the astigmatic cornea may be more comfortable than a regular hard lens. Such contacts have an "up" and a "down" to them. That is, they are heavier on the bottom than at the top. And once they are placed in the eyes, they rotate until they are in the proper position. But even these lenses do not work for all astigmatisms. A more recent development is the soft contact lens designed for astigmatism. These lenses also have an up and a down to them. In the case of soft lenses, however, the lower edge—which is usually cut straight across rather than curved—must be placed at the bottom of the cornea when the lens is inserted. This is because soft lenses are less likely to shift position in the eye than hard lenses.

Corneal astigmatisms are particularly severe and cannot be corrected with eyeglasses or contact lenses. An ophthalmologist may recommend an operation called a corneal transplant, which entails removing the patient's badly scarred cornea and replacing it with the smooth, clear cornea of someone who has recently died and donated his or her corneas for transplantation.

Strabismus, or cross-eyed or wall-eyed vision, occurs when the eyes are not parallel. The earlier the condition is detected, the more likely treatment will prove successful.

STRABISMUS AND AMBLYOPIA

Although most people consider being cross-eyed a funny notion, to some people the condition is a medical reality doctors call strabismus. Actually, strabismus means more than just being cross-eyed. Strabismus is a condition in which the two eyes do not move together. Usually the muscles of one eye are weak. Generally, one eye looks straight ahead while the other wanders inward toward the nose (cross-eye, or esotropia), or outward toward the side of the head (walleye, or exotropia). Occasionally, the weaker eye may turn upward (hypertropia) or downward (hypotropia). Strabismus can be inherited or caused by an illness or injury. It often presents itself in young children who are extremely farsighted but can also occur because the vision in one eye is much worse than the vision in the other.

If strabismus is not corrected, the child may lose much or all of the sight in the weaker eye, developing amblyopia ("lazy eye"). This is because the brain receives two very different visual images—one from the stronger eye, another from the "wandering" eye. If such a condition persists, the brain will learn to suppress the image from the wandering eye, causing that eye to develop slowly and incorrectly. Amblyopia can also occur without strabismus, simply because the vision in one eye is much worse than the vision in the other. In such a case, the brain will also try to suppress the image from the weaker eye. In either case, if the amblyopic eye is not treated in time, it may become legally blind—at best, seeing at a distance of 20 feet what the normal eye would be able to see from 200 feet away. (This is known as 20/200 vision.) And the amblyopic eye may not even have good central vision: It may not even be possible to use that eye for reading. For this reason, all babies should have their eyes examined soon after birth and again when they are six months old. In addition, children should receive an eye exam before they enter kindergarten and continue to receive regular eye exams while they are growing up. Of course, if they seem to be having visual problems, they should be examined as soon as possible.

How can strabismus or amblyopia be corrected? If the reason for the amblyopia is that one eye has much poorer vision than the other, eyeglasses or contact lenses may correct the problem. Eyeglasses can also be used, in some cases, to keep a "wandering" eye in line with the stronger eye.

In many cases, the weaker eye may need strengthening. This can usually be accomplished by placing a patch over the stronger eye, thereby forcing the weaker eye to do all the seeing for several weeks, months, or even a year. This method works best when the child is under three, but it has been successful in children as old as six. In some cases, eye drops can be used to make the vision in the good eye blurry by dilating the retina, so that the weaker eye must be used for seeing. But this method does not usually work as well as patching does.

If eyeglasses (or contact lenses), patching, or eye medication do not solve the problem, surgery may be necessary to make the eye muscles work together. Special eye exercises, along with the surgery, may help the youngster learn how to coordinate his or her eye movements.

COLOR BLINDNESS

In order to understand how color-blind people see the world, one should remember that the normal eye is sensitive to three basic colors of light—red, blue, and green. This is because the retina of the normal eye has three different types of cones: cones sensitive to red light, cones sensitive to blue light, and cones sensitive to green light. And all the other colors people see are composed of combinations of these three colors. This means that if a person cannot see one of these colors of light, he or she will also not see the colors that are made by combining this particular color of light with the other two primary colors of light.

For example, the major type of color blindness is called dichromasy. People with this condition have cones for only two of the three primary colors of light. One of the most common forms of dichromasy is protanopia, which is red blindness. Protanopes are not only unable to see reds; they cannot see colors that are mixtures of red-plus-blue or red-plus-green light. That is, red plus blue would appear blue, and red plus green would appear green.

For this reason, protanopes are unable to see oranges (which are mixtures of red and yellow light). They also have trouble distinguishing certain shades of green (e.g., yellow green) that are really mixtures of red and green light. In fact, all of the colors that are really mixtures of red and green light—including certain shades of red—will appear to the protanope as some shade of green. In addition, since white light is actually a mixture of red, blue, and green light, protanopes are unable to tell the difference between white (red plus blue plus green) and bluish green (blue plus green).

Another type of dichromasy is deuteranopia. Deuteranopes are green blind. This means that they can see neither green nor mixtures of green. Like protanopes, deuteranopes are also unable to see oranges (since these are mixtures of red and yellow lights). And they cannot tell the difference between pure reds and mixtures of red plus green that are seen as shades of green by people who have perfect color vision. So, like the protanopes, the deuteranopes confuse reds and greens. Therefore, both protanopes and deuteranopes are classified as red-green blind. But, unlike the protanopes, the deuteranopes are unable to tell the difference between white (red plus blue plus green) and purple (blue plus red).

The third type of dichromasy is tritanopia. Tritanopes are blue blind. Tritanopia is extremely rare, and most people afflicted with it have other visual problems as well. Tritanopes cannot tell the difference between purple and red or between blue green and green. And because tritanopes are blue blind, they cannot tell the difference between white (red plus blue plus green) and yellow (red plus green).

Few people are completely color-blind, lacking the ability to see any colors at all. Such people, who see no difference between the scenes on a black-and-white TV set and the world outside, are said to have achromatic vision—vision without color.

Almost all people who are color-blind are born that way. Except for a few cases caused by an eye disease later in life, it is an inherited disorder. And men are approximately eight times more likely to be color-blind than are women. Women, however, can carry the gene for color blindness and pass it along to their offspring. A daughter who inherits one gene for color blindness will also be a carrier but will not be color-blind herself. But a son who inherits the gene for color blindness from his mother will be color-blind. (A man can inherit the gene for color blindness only from his mother. Therefore, color blindness is called a sex-linked trait.) A woman becomes a carrier of color blindness if she inherits the gene from either her mother or her father. Unlike men, who need to inherit only one gene for color blindness, a woman needs to inherit two genes—one from each parent—to have the condition herself. Therefore, a woman can be color-blind (barring rare disorders) only if her father is color-blind and her mother is either a carrier of the gene for color blindness or is color-blind herself.

Although color blindness cannot be "cured," special contact lenses have helped people with the condition tell the difference between various colors they would not otherwise be able to distinguish. Also, because certain objects, such as different-colored traffic signals, are generally designed with the red and green lights in standardized positions, color-blind people are not necessarily hampered by their inability to distinguish red and green: They can tell whether to "stop" or "go" by the position, rather than the color, of the lights.

There are a number of different tests to determine whether people are color-blind. Often these tests consist of locating shapes made up of colored dots that are "buried" in a "sea" of dots of other colors. Degrees of color blindness vary. Some people (known as anomalous trichromates) can detect all three primary colors of light but have more trouble with one color than with the others. Such tests can not only tell if a person is color-blind to certain colors but can determine the extent of the condition as well.

•　　　•　　　•　　　•

CHAPTER 5

CATARACTS

A cataract operation in India

A cataract is a cloudy formation within the lens of the eye. Actually, few people's eyes have perfectly clear lenses. In fact, many people have one or more very tiny cloudy or milky-colored patches in the lenses of their eyes that do not interfere with their vision and may never cause visual problems. A cataract forms when one of the patches grows larger or denser or when a new patch grows, making seeing difficult and sometimes virtually impossible.

Normally, cataracts do not cause tearing or pain. (In rare cases, however, the cataract may swell and become painful.) The patient does notice, however, that his or her vision is getting worse. In some cases the growing cataract may at first increase the lens's refractive (bending) power so that the patient becomes more nearsighted and such close tasks as reading become easier. This type of cataract, known as a nuclear cataract, is responsible for what has been called the "second sight" of the elderly. Unfortunately, as the cataract continues to grow, vision worsens. At this point, the patient should certainly see a doctor. Slowly worsening vision is often a sign of a cataract but can also be a symptom of a much more serious condition, glaucoma. Unlike vision lost because of cataracts, vision lost because of glaucoma cannot be restored at a later time. Glaucoma should be treated as soon as possible in order to preserve whatever sight is left. (For more on glaucoma, see Chapter 6.)

Most people with cataracts are older adults. According to the National Society to Prevent Blindness, cataracts are responsible "for one out of every seven cases of blindness among persons 45 [or older]." And almost everyone over the age of 65 has some clouding of the lens that interferes with vision.

Cataracts are not limited to the elderly, however. Newborn babies are also susceptible. Cataracts found in newborns may be caused by a disease the mother had when pregnant. For example,

One-hundred-eleven-year-old Willie Guy was nearly blind in one eye until he underwent two cataract operations, in which new lenses were surgically implanted.

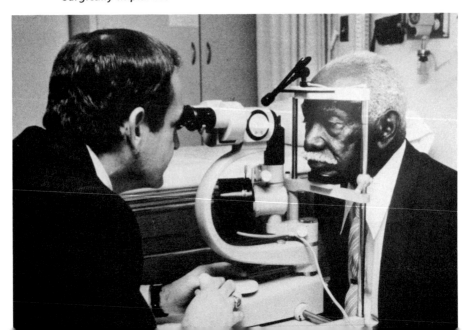

a baby may be born with cataracts if the mother had rubella (German measles) while she was carrying the baby. The earlier rubella occurs in a pregnancy, the more likely the infant is to have severe cataracts. Cataracts in infants may also be caused by a problem the infant has in properly metabolizing certain substances (using them for energy and growth). For example, if the infant is unable to metabolize galactose (a sugar) because he or she lacks the special enzyme (body chemical) that normally breaks galactose down, the lens of the eye may wind up absorbing too much water. As excess water is absorbed in the lens, it becomes more and more difficult for light to pass through. The lens becomes less and less transparent, leading to a galactose cataract.

Physical injuries, such as puncture wounds to the eye, can also cause cataracts; so can injuries caused by chemicals hitting the eye or by exposure to excessive X rays, intense heat, or other radiation, such as ultraviolet light. Even diseases, such as diabetes, and medications, such as steroids, can lead to the formation of cataracts. Scar tissue left after an injury to the lens may lead to a cataract because it disrupts the regular pattern of fibers that make up the normal, transparent lens. But scientists do not yet know what causes most of the cataracts in older people.

Cataracts may take years to form—and in some people they never become serious enough to interfere significantly with vision—or they may worsen rapidly over a few months' time. People with cataracts suffer from blurred or hazy vision. They may also see spots in front of their eyes, or they may even "see double." They may also find that lights are either too bright—especially at night—or not bright enough, especially when they are trying to do close work. And they may get no relief even when they acquire new eyeglasses. The sole procedure by which to restore sight lost because of a cataract is removal of the cloudy lens.

SURGERY

According to the National Society to Prevent Blindness, cataract surgery is successful more than 95% of the time. It can be performed in a number of different ways. The doctor may make a small incision in the cornea with a scalpel and remove the lens of the eye in one piece. In some cases, the lens is cut loose with

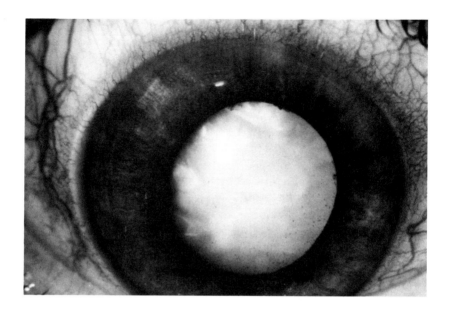

Above: *A dense cataract.* Below: *The vision of a person with such a cataract becomes blurred.*

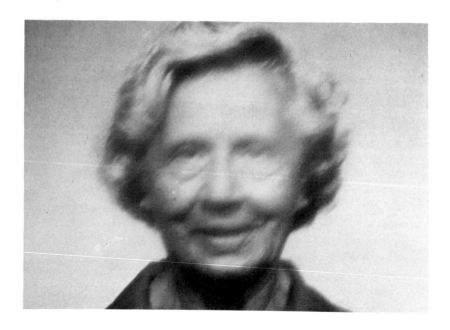

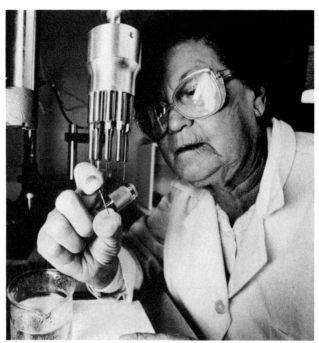

The ultrasonic tip of the Kelman Phaco-Emulsifier creates sound waves to dissolve cataracts, which are then removed by suction.

the scalpel. In other cases, special chemical substances called enzymes are used to loosen the lens. The lens may then be removed in a single piece with surgical implements or by using cryogenics—ultracold. A special instrument chilled to about −40 degrees Fahrenheit, is placed against the lens and freezes to it. The doctor then simply removes the lens with the ultracold probe. Or the lens may first be broken apart with an ultrasonic needle (an instrument that vibrates at a pitch too high for the human ear to hear) and then suctioned out.

Once the cataract is removed, light can pass through to the retina again, but vision will not be clear unless the light is focused. And it cannot be focused unless the lens that was removed is replaced in some way. That replacement can be in the form of special eyeglasses, contact lenses, or an intraocular lens (a lens that is permanently put into the eye to replace the lens that was removed).

EYEGLASSES AND CONTACT LENSES

Eyeglasses may seem to be the simplest solution, but cataract glasses are not like other eyeglasses. Cataract eyeglasses act like magnifying lenses; they make everything appear about 30%

larger than normal. Cataract glasses are also quite thick and distort peripheral vision. In order to see clearly, a person who uses such glasses needs to look through the center of the lenses. And cataract glasses may cause major problems for patients who have had cataract surgery on only one eye. If only one eye needs a cataract lens, the brain will have trouble trying to make sense of the fact that the two eyes are receiving two different-size images. (Remember that the eye that looks through the cataract eyeglasses will see things greatly magnified.) Even so, some people can eventually get used to such glasses.

Contact lenses for cataract patients cause fewer visual problems than glasses. Such lenses magnify everything by only about 6% to 8% rather than 30%. And they do not distort peripheral vision the way cataract eyeglasses do. However, not everyone can wear contact lenses; many find them unbearably uncomfortable. In addition, they are tiny, and older patients may have trouble handling them if they have arthritis or if their hands shake. They may also have more trouble finding a lost or dropped lens than other people. Fortunately, extended-wear contact lenses can give cataract patients good vision and only need to be handled once every few days or weeks.

Intraocular Implants

Most cataract patients now get intraocular implants after cataract-removal surgery. They can be inserted in the same position as the natural lens either at the time of cataract-removal surgery or at a later date. Such lenses, sitting in the "right" position, provide better vision than eyeglasses or contact lenses can. However, these artificial lenses cannot change shape the way the eye's natural lens does when it accommodates for changes in viewing near or distant objects. Therefore, even with intraocular lens implants, cataract patients may need additional eyeglasses for reading or for distance vision. Unfortunately, intraocular implants will not work for all patients, and some people have problems that require the implants to be removed. However, for the majority of patients, intraocular implants provide the most natural—and comfortable—vision after cataract surgery.

•　　　•　　　•　　　•

GLAUCOMA

Glaucoma diminishes vision gradually and painlessly.

Glaucoma occurs when pressure builds up inside the eye. If left unchecked, this high pressure can damage the retina and the optic nerve, ultimately resulting in blindness.

According to the National Society to Prevent Blindness, about 12% to 14% of all blindness in the United States is caused by glaucoma. Yet most of the afflicted people did not have to go blind, because glaucoma can generally be treated with eye drops, pills, or, in some cases, surgery. But in order for treatment to be effective, the progress of glaucoma needs to be arrested in time. Once part of a person's vision is lost to glaucoma, it cannot be recovered. And because most cases of glaucoma erode sight slowly and painlessly, the victims may be unaware that they have a problem until the glaucoma is rather advanced. That is why it is so important to have regular eye exams (at least one every two years) that include one or more tests for glaucoma. And that is why it is crucial for glaucoma patients to take their medication on a regular schedule. If they are unable to, the medication may not work as it should, and their eyesight may further erode.

Glaucoma occurs when the normal fluid that nourishes the front of the eyeball—the aqueous humor—builds up inside the eye. This usually happens because the normal drainage system that allows the aqueous humor to flow out of the eye and into the bloodstream becomes blocked. As fluid pressure continues to build in the front of the eye, it pushes on and causes damage to the retina and optic nerve. Usually, the pressure buildup occurs gradually, and eyesight is slowly and painlessly destroyed. But sometimes pressure buildup can occur quite rapidly, causing pain and requiring emergency treatment in order to save the sight in the affected eye. The two most common types of glaucoma are chronic glaucoma and acute glaucoma.

CHRONIC GLAUCOMA

Chronic glaucoma, also known as open-angle glaucoma, is the most common form of the condition. According to Arthur Freese's book *The Miracle of Vision*, between 80% and 90% of all glaucoma sufferers have this form of the disease. Chronic glaucoma usually strikes people over the age of 35, but younger people may also be affected. Glaucoma is not contagious but may be hereditary. Other people who have a higher-than-normal risk for developing chronic glaucoma include diabetics, blacks, those with a history of eye injuries or eye surgery, and people who take the medicine cortisone.

Chronic glaucoma usually has no symptoms—at least until noticeable damage has been done to the victim's vision. As time goes on and the victim's intraocular pressure (the pressure inside the eye) continues to be higher than normal, more and more of his or her peripheral vision is lost. If the glaucoma is left unchecked, the victim's visual field will become limited to a narrow "tunnel," and then, finally, all vision will be lost in the affected eye.

There is little reason, however, for chronic glaucoma to go undetected. An eye doctor can easily test for elevated intraocular pressure by using a tonometer. The simplest kind of tonometer is the indentation tonometer. In order to use this type of tonometer, the ophthalmologist must first put eye drops in the patient's eyes to anesthetize them (make them temporarily insensitive to pain). Then the doctor employs a simple plungerlike device to "walk across" the eyeball, pressing on it in one or more places. The eyeball's resistance to the doctor's attempt to push it slightly inward indicates to the ophthalmologist whether the pressure inside the eyeball is elevated. Using this

An eye doctor tests her patient for glaucoma. Because this disease does not have noticeable symptoms until it is in its advanced stages, regular tests are the only way to detect it early.

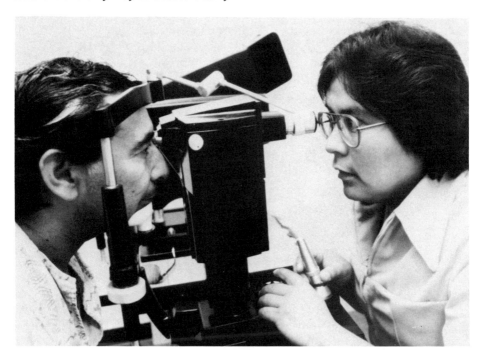

technique can determine whether or not the patient might have glaucoma. Many eye doctors now use a more complex tonometer, known as the applanation tonometer. With the applanation tonometer, the patient looks through one end of a long tube as the doctor does so through the other. As the doctor examines the patient's eye with the aid of a microscope that is part of this device, he or she will also ascertain how much pressure is required to push down part of the cornea. Still another type of tonometer tests intraocular pressure by blowing a puff of air at the cornea and measuring the resistance. Tonometer tests that do not require the use of anesthetizing eye drops can also be performed by optometrists.

If the tonometer tests show high intraocular pressure, other tests should also be performed to check for the presence of glaucoma, since a tonometer test that indicates elevated pressure is not absolute proof of the disease. In addition, the doctor may wish to test the patient's visual field and examine the optic nerve for any possible damage. He or she may also determine how well aqueous humor is draining from the eye.

Although chronic glaucoma is often present without symptoms, if a person experiences one or more of the following problems, he or she should see an eye doctor immediately.

- Problems with vision that are not helped even by frequent changes in eyeglass prescription.
- Problems adapting to darkened rooms (e.g., movie theaters) and/or the need to use increasingly brighter lights in order to see well. Also, problems seeing well when driving at night.
- Loss of peripheral vision.
- Blurry vision.
- Seeing rainbow-colored rings around lights.

Treating Chronic Glaucoma

Generally, chronic glaucoma can be controlled with eye drops or ointment. Sometimes the ophthalmologist will prescribe more than one kind of eye drop or a combination of eye drops and ointment for the glaucoma patient. In addition, the patient may need to take pills to control the production of aqueous humor. These medicines need to be taken on time and according to the ophthalmologist's directions in order to control the pressure inside the eye. For patients who have trouble with eye drops, there are also time-release medications available on tiny hemispherical contact-lens-like discs that can be placed under the lower eyelid. These tiny "medicine dispensers" allow medication to be released slowly and regularly, providing for constant control of the patient's intraocular pressure. A glaucoma patient may also need to see the ophthalmologist every few months in order to ensure that the medication is working properly.

Eye-drop medications used to control chronic glaucoma include pilocarpine, carbachol, and timolol. Patients taking medication for glaucoma should inform their other physicians about the glaucoma medication they are taking so that the latter do not prescribe medications that might either raise the patient's intraocular pressure or interfere with the effectiveness of their glaucoma medication. If medication does not control the patient's glaucoma by either slowing aqueous production (timolol) or increasing the rate of fluid drainage (pilocarpine and carbachol), an operation may be necessary to allow aqueous humor to flow out of the eye more quickly.

If surgery should become necessary, an eye surgeon may decide to enlarge the eye's natural drainage channel or to create a new channel to rid the eye of excess aqueous humor. Alternatively, the surgeon may implant a special valve that works like a "trapdoor" so that fluid drains from the eye. Still another possibility is to use a cold probe to freeze part of the aqueous-producing mechanism so that the production of aqueous humor is permanently reduced.

ACUTE GLAUCOMA

Acute glaucoma, also known as narrow-angle or angle-closure glaucoma, is the other major type of the disease, affecting about 10% of all glaucoma sufferers. Acute glaucoma occurs when the iris of the eye is suddenly pushed forward, blocking the eye's

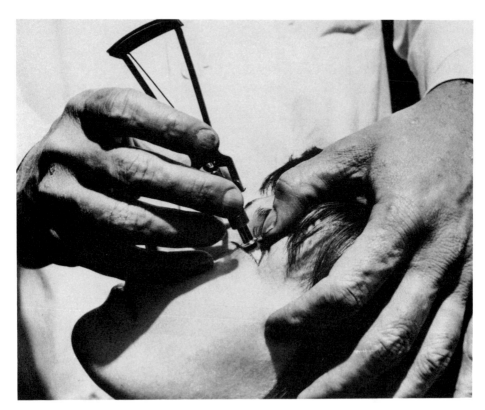

A tonometer checks eye pressure and is a preliminary test for glaucoma. Treatments for chronic glaucoma may include eye drops, drugs, ointments, or surgery.

fluid-drainage channel. With the channel blocked, fluid pressure builds up very rapidly, causing severe pain, often accompanied by nausea and vomiting. Vision becomes blurred, and the victim may see colored rings around lights. The eye may become red and feel as hard as a rock. Acute glaucoma can cause permanent damage to the retina and optic nerve in just a few hours' time. So, as with any other medical emergency, the victim should be rushed to the hospital immediately. If possible, both the hospital and the victim's ophthalmologist should be notified of the acute glaucoma attack so that treatment can begin as soon as the patient reaches the hospital. Medication to lower intraocular pressure should be given as soon as possible. This may be sufficient to stop the attack for the moment, but most people who have had an attack of acute glaucoma will need surgery on the affected eye to prevent a recurrence. The surgery, known as an iridectomy, involves using a scalpel or laser beam to cut a tiny hole in the iris to allow the aqueous humor to escape. This may solve the patient's problem permanently, or additional surgery may be needed to fix the eye's natural drainage channel as well. Because many people who have had an attack of acute glaucoma in one eye eventually have the same problem with the other one, many ophthalmologists recommend that the unaffected eye undergo an iridectomy as a preventive measure. An attack of acute glaucoma may precipitate by itself, or it may result from a blow to the head or prolonged dilation of the pupil (either by extended exposure to the dark or during an eye exam when drops to dilate the pupil are used). Even emotional upset has been known to trigger an attack.

If a person's parents, brothers or sisters, or another relative has had an attack of acute glaucoma, he or she is more likely to suffer one as well. Others who have a higher-than-normal risk for developing acute glaucoma include people who are extremely farsighted and those whose eyes have a much shallower-than-normal anterior chamber.

If a person experiences either of the following problems, he or she should contact a doctor immediately. They may be warning signs of a future attack of acute glaucoma:

- Seeing rainbow-colored rings around lights.
- Having repeated headaches around the eyes.

In addition, even patients who have had surgery for acute glaucoma are not immune to getting chronic glaucoma, so they must also have regular checkups to prevent this.

OTHER TYPES OF GLAUCOMA

The other types of glaucoma are congenital (infantile) glaucoma and secondary glaucoma. Congenital glaucoma is rare. It may be present at birth or develop within the first few months of life. The affected child may have bulging or enlarged eyes, or the eyes may seem unusually sensitive to light or tear more often than

RETINAL PROBLEMS

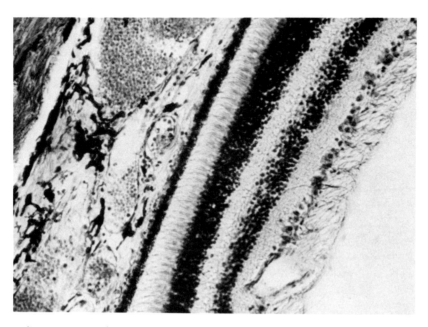

A human-eye retina

Retinitis pigmentosa (RP) is a disease that causes the retina of the eye to slowly degenerate. Early symptoms of retinitis pigmentosa can usually be detected in children or young adults. The first symptom of retinitis pigmentosa is usually night blindness (difficulty seeing in darkened rooms or outdoors at night.) Then there is a slow loss of peripheral vision. As their field of vision becomes narrower and narrower, victims of RP are left with only "tunnel vision"—a narrow central field of vision. And

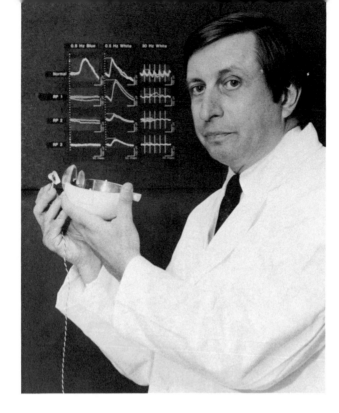

A physician displays a test for retinitis pigmentosa in which a contact lens measures and electronically records the amount of light reflected off an actual retina.

finally, usually after many years, some victims of retinitis pigmentosa may lose what is left of their central vision as well.

RP is marked by the dysfunction of the eye's rods and cones. But just what causes this to happen is not yet known. And, at the moment, there is no cure. RP is usually inherited; it is passed on to children by parents who may either have RP or carry one gene for RP. There are three different ways a child can inherit RP from his or her parents. The most common form of RP is what scientists call autosomal (not linked to a sex—X or Y— chromosome) recessive. That is, the child must inherit a gene for RP from each of his or her parents. Because the gene that is passed on is a recessive one, RP may develop in a child who has no relatives with the disease. In another form of RP, the child inherits the disease from a parent who also has RP. In this case, the gene for RP is dominant. Only one parent need have RP for the child to inherit it. Moreover, the affected parent has a 50-50 chance of having a child with RP. The third form of RP is known as "sex-linked" RP, in which the gene for RP is carried on the X chromosome. Women who inherit one RP-gene-carrying X chromosome are carriers—they do not have the disease RP, but they can transmit the RP gene to their children. Daughters who inherit an RP gene from their mothers only are also carriers. But sons who inherit an RP gene from their mothers have the disease because men can inherit sex-linked RP only from their mothers. This is because males have one X chromosome and one Y chromosome, whereas females have two X chromosomes. The non-affected X chromosome in females "protects" the carrier females from getting the disease. In the sex-linked form of RP, females inherit the disease only if they acquire two X chromosomes with the RP gene—that is, one gene for RP from each of their parents.

According to the Retinitis Pigmentosa Foundation Fighting Blindness, nearly 30% of those who have RP also have a hearing loss. When the two conditions occur together, the disorder is known as Usher's syndrome. Although the loss of vision in Usher's syndrome is progressive, as it is for others with RP, hearing does not usually get progressively worse.

If a person has RP and other members of his or her family do as well, the rate at which his or her vision deteriorates will probably be similar to the rate at which other family members have lost their eyesight. A number of low-vision aids are available to help victims of RP. There is also equipment, known as the night-vision aid, that is designed to help night-blind RP victims who still have fairly good daytime vision to get around at night. The night-vision aid electronically magnifies the intensity of the light that is reflected from objects at night. This brighter-than-life image allows the person with RP to see objects that would normally be too obscure for him or her to see.

MACULAR DEGENERATION

One of the most common causes of retinal damage is AMD (age-related macular degeneration). Unlike RP, which destroys peripheral vision first, AMD destroys the macula—the central region of the retina. It is the macula that gives people their sharpest vision. Although young people can get AMD, the disease usually affects those over 55. Arteriosclerosis (hardening of the arteries), eye injuries, and, it is theorized, heredity may be causes of AMD. According to the National Society to Prevent Blindness, AMD is the leading cause of blindness in people older than 75.

AMD comes in two forms—"wet" and "dry." Dry AMD is the more common form, progressing slowly, usually taking many

Macular degeneration causes the center of a scene to appear smudged or empty.

years to destroy the victim's vision. Currently, dry AMD cannot be arrested. However, low-vision aids may help patients in the early stages of this disease.

Unlike dry AMD, in wet AMD a large number of minute, fragile blood vessels suddenly begin to form below the retina. Because these new blood vessels are so delicate, they often break, and leaking blood causes damage to the retina. If the disorder is diagnosed early enough, laser surgery can seal the tiny blood vessels and prevent further leakages. But not all such blood vessels can be treated in this way: Those that lie too close to the fovea (the central part of the macula) cannot be treated because the laser beam, in treating those blood vessels, may also damage the fovea.

Because early detection of wet AMD is crucial to preventing further vision loss, it is imperative that the disease be detected as early as possible. In order to aid in this detection, a person should have regular eye exams and be aware of the following warning signs:

- Vertical lines, such as flagpoles, appear wavy.
- Print on a page may look blurred, or the type may not seem to be uniformly dark.
- The center of a scene may appear smudged, darkened, or empty.
- In some cases, because the region of the retina that contains the cones may be affected, color vision may be lost.

Patients can also test themselves at home with the aid of a test called the Amsler Grid, which looks like a square sheet of horizontally and vertically ruled graph paper with a black dot at the center. The Amsler Grid usually consists of black lines on a white piece of paper, but it may also be made of white lines on a black piece of paper. Each eye should be tested separately by looking at the center of the grid. If some of the lines—especially those near the central dot—appear wavy or if part of the grid seems to be missing or one section appears darker than the rest, the person may have AMD (although these symptoms can be signs of other disorders as well) and should get a thorough eye exam as soon as possible.

DIABETIC RETINOPATHY

Like the loss of vision from wet AMD, vision loss from diabetic retinopathy occurs when blood vessels leak into the eye, damaging the retina. Almost half of all people who have had diabetes for more than 15 years have at least a mild form of diabetic retinopathy. Although diabetic retinopathy may not appear in a diabetic for many years, it can also be one of the first warning signs that a person has developed diabetes. Smoking, high blood pressure, and pregnancy further aggravate this disorder.

The first symptoms of diabetic retinopathy are swelling and bulging blood vessels. As the blood vessels swell, they may leak

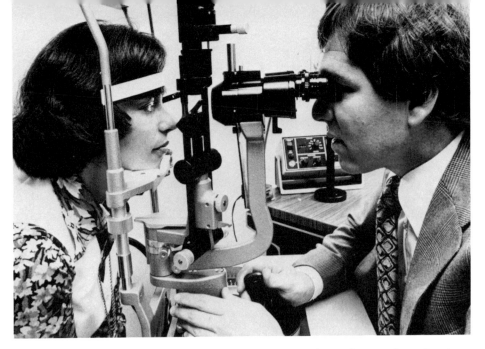

A patient with proliferative diabetic retinopathy undergoes laser treatment at the Eye Institute of New Jersey. This technique is successful more than 60% of the time.

into the retina. This can cause problems with vision. As the diabetic retinopathy worsens, the bleeding blood vessels may cause permanent damage to the retina. In addition, new blood vessels may form and bleed into the vitreous humor, interfering with vision. Scar tissue may also form on the retina and can lead to retinal tears or to a detached retina (see below).

There are several procedures that can control diabetic retinopathy. In some cases, a laser can be used to seal off the leaking blood vessels. This process is known as photocoagulation. Laser treatment can also repair retinal tears or a detached retina. When there is extensive damage to the vitreous humor, another type of surgery, called a vitrectomy, may restore vision. Vitrectomy involves removing blood spots and scar tissue that are in the vitreous humor. At the same time, the vitreous humor itself is sucked out of the eye and replaced with a clear saline (salt) solution. But early treatment is still the best way to try to prevent vision loss caused by diabetic retinopathy. The National Society to Prevent Blindness recommends that diabetics be examined by an ophthalmologist at least once a year—to try to detect any blood vessel problems before they affect vision.

RETINAL TEARS AND DETACHED RETINA

If a person sees dark spots floating in front of his or her eyes, flashes of light, or if his or her vision suddenly becomes blurred, or if, soon after, he or she sees a whole "shower" of sparks or dark spots or a "curtain" moving across the eye, obscuring vision, he or she should be rushed to a hospital immediately. These are symptoms of a detached retina, which occurs when the retina becomes separated from its underlying layer, the pigment epithelium. Generally, detached retinas occur more often in older people as the retina weakens with age. However, a severe blow to the eye or head may also cause the retina to detach. In addition, severely myopic people may be more likely to suffer from detached retinas, because their retinas tend to strain forward as they try to focus on distant objects.

Often, a detached retina begins with a small hole or a tear that forms in the retina. The hole or tear then becomes larger as fluid

A detached retina operation. This surgery is effective in nearly 85% of all cases, but follow-up treatment is essential for total recovery.

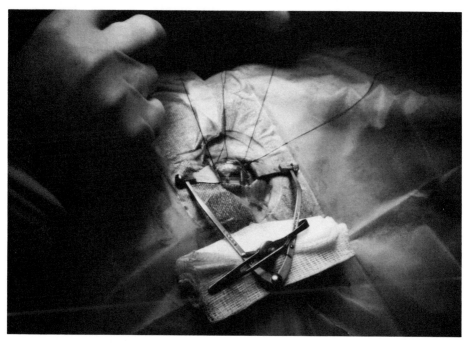

flows through it. As it grows ever larger, the hole or tear pulls the retina farther from the pigment epithelium. The dark or irregularly shaped "floaters," flashes of light, or blurred vision a person may experience are all warning signs of the impending detachment. The "shower" of sparks or dark spots, or the "curtain" moving across the eye, are symptoms of the actual detachment. A detached retina is a serious medical emergency. Although nearly 85% of the time the retina can be reattached, the procedure must be followed with treatment for it to be successful. The ophthalmologist may repair the retina with surgery by using the heat of a laser to "solder" the retina together. Or a cold probe may be used to "freeze" the retina in place. If a detached retina is not treated in time, blindness will occur in that eye.

RETINAL VEIN OCCLUSION

Retinal vein occlusion (RVO) is an eye disorder in which one or more of the veins that supply blood to the retina become blocked. When the veins become blocked, one of three things can happen: An inadequate supply of blood may reach the retina; blood from the blocked veins may leak into the retina; or the body may try to compensate for the blocked veins by forming new blood vessels. Unfortunately, any of these situations may cause damage to the retina that, in turn, can lead to partial loss of vision or to blindness. Because symptoms of RVO can develop without the subject's noticing any problems at first, it is important to test the vision of each eye separately. If additional blood vessels have formed as a result of RVO, they can sometimes be prevented from causing further vision loss by use of laser surgery. RVO patients should also see their family doctors, because retinal vein occlusion may be a sign of high blood pressure, diabetes, or heart disease.

•   •   •   •

CHAPTER 8

OTHER DISORDERS OF THE EYE

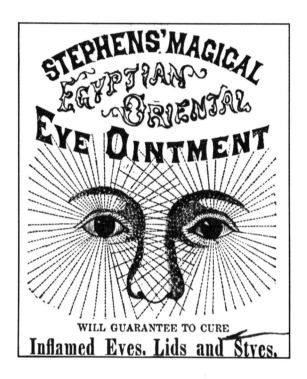

STEPHENS' MAGICAL EGYPTIAN ORIENTAL EYE OINTMENT

WILL GUARANTEE TO CURE

Inflamed Eyes. Lids and Styes.

There are a number of common disorders that affect the eye temporarily and can be effectively treated and cured. Perhaps the most common is conjunctivitis. More popularly known as "pinkeye," conjunctivitis is an inflammation of the conjunctiva usually caused by allergy or infection. Symptoms include itching and redness, watery and painful eyes, and the presence of pus. Conjunctivitis caused by a viral or bacterial infection can be spread by casual contact from one person to another and should be treated by an ophthalmologist. Exposure to very bright lights, such as bright sunlight on new snow, or the light from a welding tool or sunlamp can also cause the condition.

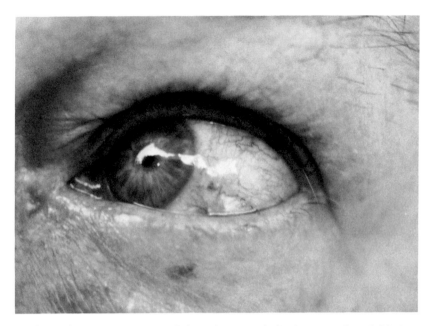

Perhaps the most common of the minor eye irritations, conjunctivitis is easily treatable with proper medication.

AGE AND EYE DISORDERS

Corneal problems that affect people as they age include bullous keratopathy and keratoconus. Bullous keratopathy is caused by excess fluid buildup in the cornea. The excess fluid can cause pain and visual problems. The condition can sometimes be treated with medication that decreases the fluid buildup or by wearing soft contact lenses (which absorb fluid from the eye). In some cases, corneal transplants are indicated.

Keratoconus is a condition that usually develops during the teenage years, or soon before. Keratoconus causes the cornea to become cone shaped, and that "cone" becomes more pointed as the patient ages. These changes in the shape of the cornea cause increasing nearsightedness. There may also be corneal astigmatism (blurring of vision caused by an irregularly shaped cornea scattering the light rays entering the eye rather than allowing them to come to a single focus at the retina) that worsens with time. Eye doctors should carefully examine extremely nearsighted and extremely astigmatic patients to determine whether these problems might be due to keratoconus. Hard contact lenses may help keep the cornea flat, but such lenses may be difficult or impossible to wear if there is extensive corneal astigmatism. (This is because the contact lens would have to ride on a "bumpy" cornea.) However, if the cornea becomes extremely pointed and thin, or scarred, surgery may be necessary. In some cases, corneal transplants may be required to restore vision.

FLOATERS

Everyone occasionally sees tiny dark spots or long, slender, trans-lucent threadlike "wigglers" in front of their eyes. Very near-sighted people and older adults, however, may see them more often. Such "floaters" are more noticeable when viewed against a pale surface. Also, people who are nearsighted and/or astig-matic may see them "dancing" in distant streetlights at night if they look at them without their glasses. In most cases, floaters are not a cause for alarm. Generally, they are simply cells or debris floating around in the person's eyes, and they usually dis-appear after a short time. However, a person should alert his or her eye doctor to these floaters, for they can turn out to be a symptom of a more serious disorder, such as a detached retina. In addition, if there is an abrupt increase in spots or a person suddenly sees flashes of light, he or she should contact an ophthalmologist at once.

STIES

A sty usually looks like a tiny pimple forming at the base of an eyelash. They are usually superficial, although some sties are deeper and may affect one or more glands of the eye. Sties are generally caused by bacterial infection. Although warm, moist compresses may help eliminate the sty, antibiotic eye drops are often needed. Occasionally, antibiotic pills may also be necessary to stop the infection.

EYELID PROBLEMS

Older people often suffer from drooping or improperly positioned eyelids. Malpositioned eyelids may be turned inward so that the lashes rub the cornea and cause scarring. Or the eyelids may

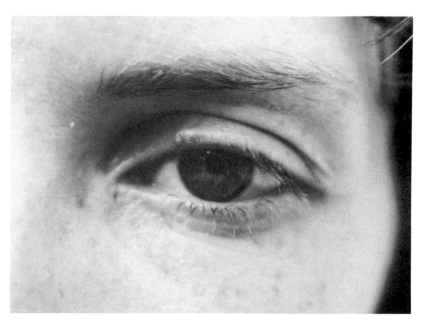

Sties, which usually result from a bacterial infection, are treated with a combination of antibiotics and warm compresses.

"relax" with age so that the tears, instead of draining properly, overflow the eye. Problems associated with this drooping eyelid include skin irritation and redness. Plastic surgery can stop the lids from drooping or turning inward.

TEARING PROBLEMS

Dry eye is a common complaint among older people. Although to many people it may sound like a minor annoyance, it can grow serious if left untreated. If left unchecked, the cornea can become dry, translucent, or opaque (instead of transparent) and can interfere with vision. Dry eyes occur when the tear glands fail to produce an adequate amount of tears to lubricate the cornea properly. Sometimes eye drops or "artificial tears" help. Other times, surgery may be needed to tighten the eyelids or to block regions from which the tears may be leaking.

But more tears are not what every older person needs. Sometimes the problem is just the reverse—watery eyes. At best, the condition is annoying; at worst, it can be dangerous. Watery eyes can be caused by inflammation (redness, swelling, heat, and pain that is the body's response to an injury) or ulcerations (breaks in the tissue), which can become infected. Watery eyes can also result if the tear canals—which drain tears from the eyes through the nose and throat—become blocked. Fortunately, blocked tear canals can be fixed by a simple operation.

OTHER PROBLEMS

Older people are also more likely to develop yellow "bumps" or nodules on the nasal side and on the outer edge of the cornea. These nodules may be caused by excessive exposure to wind and dust and normally, they are nothing to be concerned about. If, however, the nodules grow larger, are uncomfortable, or make seeing difficult (which is more likely to happen to people living in hot, dusty climates), they should be removed by an eye surgeon.

BLINDNESS

There are a number of reasons why a person loses his or her sight. In many cases it is often a question of inadequate or late medical attention. In any case, there are a number of conditions

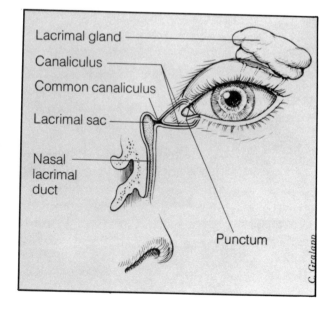

Eye irritations stimulate the lachrymal gland to produce tears. This liquid enters the eye through the punctum, drains through the canaliculus, enters the lachrymal sac, and then trickles down the nasal lachrymal duct into the nose.

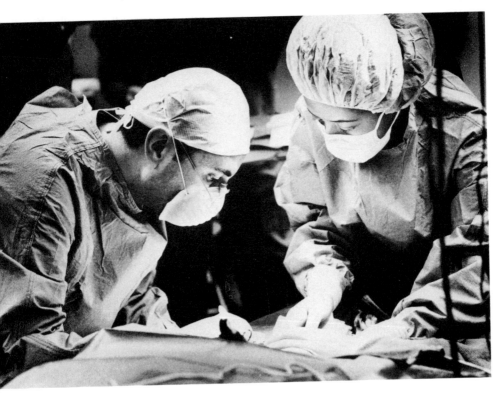

Eye surgeons implant a tiny plastic telescope to restore vision in the eye of a man who was blinded by a severe drug reaction that dried up the mucous membranes in his body and scarred his eyes.

and disorders that can lead to blindness as well as a number of precautions that can be taken to prevent it. The following section includes some of these disorders as well as some of the possible preventions against blindness.

Trachoma

Trachoma is a leading cause of blindness in developing countries. It is caused by a bacterium, Chlamydia trachomatis, and is easily spread from one person to another by sharing contaminated towels or other objects that have come in contact with an infected eye. Trachoma causes tearing, eyelid swelling, and oversensitivity to light and damages the tear ducts, eyelid, conjunctiva, and cornea. If treatment is given early enough, corneal scarring and blindness can be prevented. Antibiotics, in the form of eye drops, pills or ointments, can usually stop the progress of the disease.

Sun Damage

Sun can cause a great deal of damage to the human body. In addition to the havoc it can wreak on the skin, the sun can injure the delicate parts of the eye. Looking directly at the sun (even during a total solar eclipse) can cause retinal burns and permanent eye damage—even blindness. Likewise, using a sunlamp without adequate eye protection can also damage eyes. In addition, bright sunlight reflecting off ice or newly fallen snow can cause a condition known as snow blindness. This is caused by the sun's ultraviolet light—the same light that can cause sunburn. Wearing dark glasses can help protect eyes from sun damage, but only if they are designed to screen out both long- and short-wave ultraviolet light as well as infrared (heat) radiation. It is important that sunglasses screen out the radiation, because wearing dark glasses will cause the pupils to dilate (expand), allowing in higher levels of light. If excess, invisible ultraviolet and infrared radiation gets through, the eyes may suffer permanent damage. In other words, the wrong sunglasses may be worse than no sunglasses at all. Gray, "smoke"-color, green, or brown lenses are best, and the lenses should be large enough to keep eyes well protected. Safety glasses should always be used for sports or outdoor work.

Cosmetic Dangers

Although many cosmetics, particularly eye makeup, contain special germ-killing chemicals, in some cases their use may cause infection. This can be especially dangerous if the eye makeup in question is eyeliner or mascara. Mascara, in particular, may become tainted after four to six months of use, and if the cornea is scratched with a wand from such a bottle of mascara, the eye may become infected. For this reason, eye makeup should never be shared or kept past a few months. In addition, makeup should be applied only when the eye is closed and should never be put directly into the eye—as is the case with some liners that are used on the inner eyelids.

Special Care of Contact Lenses

A new concern for contact-lens wearers—especially for those who wear soft contact lenses—is an infection known as Acanthamoeba keratitis (uh-KAN-thuh-ME-buh kar-uh-TIE-tis). Acanthamoeba keratitis is a hard-to-treat eye disease caused by tiny creatures called amoebas that live in water and soil. *Acanthamoeba* can also live in unsterile saline solutions. Bottled saline solutions found in the store have been sterilized. Some contain preservatives, but others do not and must be used immediately after opening. (Such solutions should never be saved once their single-use bottles are opened.) But many soft-contact-lens wearers (and some hard-lens wearers) make their own saline solutions from distilled water and salt tablets. Such solutions cannot be assumed to be sterile and should be used only for boiling the lenses. Unboiled homemade saline solution must never be used as eye drops or for rinsing lenses just before they are inserted into the eyes. Those who do so risk getting bacterial or *Acanthamoeba* infections, warned researchers from the Centers for Disease Control in a July 1987 press release. These amoebas need bacteria in order to survive. And, says Richard Lippman, director of the FDA's (Food and Drug Administration) Division of Ophthalmic Devices, if there is a scratch on the cornea and it becomes infected with bacteria, the amoebas can take hold there. Although cases of Acanthamoeba keratitis are rare, they can be confused with other eye infections, delaying proper treatment. And the longer an Acanthamoeba keratitis infection goes untreated, the more difficult it will be to control.

Acanthamoeba infections can cause partial or complete blindness. In some cases, corneal transplants may be needed to preserve a patient's sight. But such transplants are not always successful. To ensure that bacteria will not breed in saline solution or on lenses, contact-lens wearers should always remember to wash their hands before handling their lenses and to use only sterile solutions. Soft-lens wearers should be particularly careful, as soft lenses absorb water and therefore whatever chemicals and/or bacteria it contains.

Protective Eyewear

Young people and adults playing a team sport such as basketball, hockey, football, or volleyball or engaging in a sport such as swimming or even a job or hobby such as chemistry or wood shop should always wear safety eye wear.

Thousands of people are victims of eye injuries each year from various sports-related accidents. Many others suffer eye injuries on the job. Although such work-related injuries may cause some sort of permanent visual loss to the victim, many accidents could have been prevented if only the victims had used safety glasses or goggles made of polycarbonate.

According to the National Society to Prevent Blindness, people who participate in moderate- to high-risk sports, such as racket sports (tennis, racketball, squash, badminton), hockey, lacrosse, baseball, football, basketball, and volleyball should wear special sports eyeglass frames with 20-millimeter polycarbonate lenses, and some of them (catchers on a baseball team, for example) should wear face masks and helmets. People who do not need

A 16th-century etching of a man with an eye-shade. Too much exposure to the rays of the sun can damage the eyes.

glasses and those who wear contact lenses should get nonprescription polycarbonate glasses, and those with prescription glasses should have polycarbonate prescription sports glasses specially made for them. Regular glasses and plastic eyeglasses used for street wear are not suitable for sports. Neither are the lensless eye guards some people use for contact sports.

For those involved in jobs or classes that have the potential to cause eye injuries from chemical burns, flying sparks, dust, or other small objects, special eye guards, goggles, or face masks should be used. Sporting-goods stores and industrial-supply houses that produce safety equipment are good places to shop for safety eye wear. An eye doctor may also be able to supply an individual with safety eye wear or recommend a place where he or she can find what is needed. If, despite precautions, someone gets a foreign object in his or her eye, that person should try removing it by allowing his or her eye to tear or by flooding the eye with water. Objects imbedded in the eye must be removed by a physician. If chemicals should splash into a person's eye, the eye should be flooded with water immediately and the person rushed to the hospital or eye doctor.

Vitamin A

Vitamin A helps the eye make proper adjustments to changes in light levels. People who do not get enough vitamin A may suffer from night blindness. If a person goes without vitamin A for long periods of time, he or she may develop xerophthalmia. Xerophthalmia, often seen in children from developing countries, causes dry eye and can lead to blindness if left unchecked. A single dose of the proper amount of vitamin A, however, can protect such children from xerophthalmia for long periods of time.

Good sources of vitamin A include yellow, orange, and green vegetables, milk, liver, fish oils, egg yolks, and butter. Because overdoses of vitamin A can be dangerous, those individuals who require supplements should take beta carotene (which is converted by the body into vitamin A), because it is less likely to be stored in the body than standard oil-soluble vitamin A supplements.

•　　　•　　　•　　　•

CHAPTER 9

OPTICAL ILLUSIONS

Two heads or a vase?

Magicians often say that the hand is quicker than the eye. Most of their magic, however, is done through misdirection (trying to get people to look in one direction while they do something somewhere else) and illusion (making people believe that what they see is real)—for example, that a person is really sawed in half and then put back together again.

Although most people are not magicians, they can have fun with another class of illusions (some of which magicians also

Psychoactive drugs can distort vision and cause hallucinations. They can also damage eyesight permanently.

use) known as optical illusions. Many people have looked at a picture of two heads and, after staring at it for a while, have seen a vase between the two heads. Or, after looking at a picture of what at first appears to be an old hag, have watched the hag transformed into a beautiful young woman. These pictures are ambiguous; their images and meanings can be interpreted in more than one way. Other such illusions include a stairway that seems to first start at ground level, then appears to reverse direction and hang from the ceiling, and a picture of a flock of white gulls against a black background that seems to change suddenly into a picture of black fish—headed in the opposite direction—against a white background.

There are other kinds of optical illusions, too, where things appear to be a certain way, but are not really as they seem. Such an optical illusion appears when viewing, for example, two straight lines, one above the other, where one has arrowheads facing outward on each end and the other has arrowheads facing inward on each end. One of the lines appears to be longer than the other, yet when they are both measured with a ruler, it is evident that they are both the same length. Another example involves the placement of two identical images (cubes, lamps, railroad cars, etc.) on converging lines at different points on a drawing (such as a picture of railroad tracks that seem to meet in the distance). Although the images are identical, the image placed where the lines are closer together will appear larger. The apparently larger image has not been drawn to scale; it is not in perspective. And because the mind assumes that the object placed where the lines converge more is actually the more distant, it interprets the object to be larger than the other. For a similar reason, the moon appears larger when seen against the horizon—especially when the horizon seems to be quite distant—than it does when it is seen overhead.

Optical illusions can lead to problems for scientists as well. Take, for example, the difficulties they face in interpreting photographs of the moon and other planets. Unless aware of the position of the sun lighting the landscape, shadows in the picture may cause them to mistake volcanic craters for mountains.

All joking aside, a visit to the eye doctor should be an annual routine.

The motion picture is another type of optical illusion. When a person watches a movie, the action seems to be continuous. But what they are really watching is a series of still pictures shown in quick succession. Because the pictures flash by quickly enough, the person continues to see the image of one picture as the next comes into view. The mind, therefore, creates the illusion of movement from a series of still pictures. "Moving" neon signs also take advantage of this same process.

Certain psychoactive drugs—hallucinogens, for example—may also "fool" the eye by distorting vision and even produce hallucinations. Marijuana can cause its user to see fiery meteors or bright, vivid colors where there are none. Stronger hallucinogens, such as LSD, prompt an even stranger response from users. Users of these psychoactive drugs report having particular visual hallucinations, often seeing lattices, cobwebs, funnels, or spirals. In addition, users often feel their vision is heightened—they may believe that they can see the pores on someone's skin. Opiates, narcotic drugs derived from the opium poppy, can cause a disturbance in visual memory, making it more difficult for users to concentrate and remember what they have seen under the influence of the drugs.

Unfortunately, many people use and abuse psychoactive drugs simply to experience the visual distortions and accompanying side effects. Such substances are illegal, however, and can cause permanent damage to a person's sight. For this reason, it is hardly worth the price that may be paid to indulge in their use.

CONCLUSION

The sense of sight is an amazing one—one whose loss is perhaps the most difficult to adjust to. Many people, however, are forced to adjust to losing their vision as it succumbs to disease or simply age. With proper care and attention, however, loss of sight can often be averted. This entails receiving yearly checkups from a qualified eye doctor. That is a small price to pay to protect the organ essential to vision: the eye.

•   •   •   •

APPENDIX:
FOR MORE INFORMATION

The following is a list of national associations and organizations that can provide further information on disorders and diseases of the eye, visual health care issues, and services for the blind and visually impaired.

GENERAL

American Society of Cataract and
  Refractive Surgery
3702 Pender Drive
Suite 250
Fairfax, VA 22030
(703) 591-2220
(an organization of
  ophthalmologists offering
  information on anterior segment
  surgery and refractive corneal
  surgery to fellow
  ophthalmologists and the public)

Better Vision Institute
1800 North Kent Street
Suite 1210
Rosslyn, VA 22209
(703) 243-1508
(an organization of professionals
  that publishes booklets,
  pamphlets, charts, and posters
  on eye care and also produces
  educational kits for schools and
  the public)

Citizens for Eye Research
5901 West Main Street
Belleville, IL 62223
(618) 233-1130
(a voluntary organization that
  provides information concerning
  eye diseases and research; also
  keeps abreast of progress on
  congressional appropriations
  made for the National Eye
  Institute)

Division for the Visually
  Handicapped
Council for Exceptional Children
1920 Association Drive
Reston, VA 22091
(703) 620-3660

Eye Bank Association of America
1725 Eye Street NW
Suite 308
Washington, DC 20006
(202) 775-4999
(an organization of eye banks
  concerned with public education
  and donor procurement)

Foundation for Education and
Research in Vision, Inc.
P.O. Box 14170
Houston, TX 77221
(713) 749-1380
(provides financial support to
universities that teach visual care
courses; also disseminates
information on vision and visual
care to the public)

National Association for Visually
Handicapped
22 West 21st Street
New York, NY 10010
(212) 889-3141
(a voluntary health organization
that acts as an information
clearinghouse on all public and
private services available to the
partially seeing)

National Eye and Health
Foundation
899 Skokie Boulevard
Northbrook, IL 60062
(312) 564-4652
(a public information center for
questions on eye care)

National Eye Institute
Information Office
Building 31, Room 6A32
9000 Rockville Pike
Bethesda, MD 20892
(301) 496-5248
(a division of the National
Institutes of Health that provides
information on research and the
diagnosis of eye disease; is also a
Retinitis Pigmentosa Center that
receives support from the
Retinitis Pigmentosa Foundation
Fighting Blindness)

National Society to Prevent
Blindness
500 East Remington Road
Schaumburg, IL 60173

(312) 843-2020
(800) 331-2020
Hot Line: (800) 221-3004
(a voluntary health agency that
provides professional and public
education programs and
community services that promote
and support local glaucoma
screening programs, preschool
vision testing, and industrial eye
safety; also provides information
and referral services on specific
eye disorders)

DISORDERS AND DISEASE

Foundation for Glaucoma Research
490 Post Street
Suite 830
San Francisco, CA 91402
(415) 986-3162
(provides information, and grants
money to researchers and
maintains a network of support
groups)

Retinitis Pigmentosa Eye Research
Suite 411
185 Spadina Avenue
Toronto, Ontario M4T 2C6
Canada
(416) 598-4951
(disseminates information to the
public and funds research on
retinitis pigmentosa and retinal
degeneration)

Retinitis Pigmentosa Foundation
Fighting Blindness
1401 Mount Royal Avenue
4th Floor
Baltimore, MD 21217
(800) 638-2300
(301) 225-9400
(provides information to the public,
conducts human service
programs, and funds research
internationally)

SERVICE TO THE BLIND

American Council of the Blind
1010 Vermont Avenue NW
Suite 1100
Washington, DC 20005
(202) 393-3666
(800) 424-8666
(consumer organization of blind
and visually impaired persons;
serves as a national information
clearinghouse on blindness for
organizations, institutions, and
the public)

American Foundation for the Blind
15 West 16th Street
New York, NY 10011
(212) 620-2000
Hot Line: (800) AF-BLIND
(a clearinghouse for local and
regional agencies; concerned
with research, information, and
consultation)

American Printing House for the
Blind
P.O. Box 6085
Louisville, KY 40206-0085
(502) 895-2405
(produces educational aids and
literature for the visually
impaired and maintains a
reference catalog service for
students)

Association for Education and
Rehabilitation of the Blind and
Visually Impaired
206 North Washington Street #320
Alexandria, VA 22314
(703) 548-1884
(provides employment information
and maintains a reference
information center)

Canadian Council of the Blind
96 Ridout Street, South
London, Ontario N6C 3X4
Canada
(519) 434-4339

(affiliation of blind persons
concerned with the rehabilitation
of the blind)

Canadian National Institute for the
Blind
1931 Bayview Avenue
Toronto, Ontario N4G 4C8
Canada
(416) 480-7580

Council of Citizens with Low Vision
1400 North Drake Road #218
Kalamazoo, MI 49007
(616) 381-9566
(an advocacy membership
organization that promotes
research and development of
professional training in low
vision, establishes outreach
programs, and provides
information to the public)

National Association for Parents of
the Visually Impaired
P.O. Box 562
Camden, NY 13316
(315) 245-3442
(800) 562-6265
(a nonprofit organization that
provides support to families
through local and state groups;
also acts as a national
clearinghouse for information
and referrals)

National Federation of the Blind
1800 Johnson Street
Baltimore, MD 21230
(301) 659-9314
(800) 638-7518: Job Opportunities
for the Blind Program
(federation of state and local
organizations of blind people;
monitors legislation, evaluates
programs for the blind, and
promotes needed services; also
distributes information to the
public)

Vision Foundation
818 Mount Auburn Street
Watertown, MA 02172
(617) 926-4232
(self-help organization for the
blind; provides a national
information referral service)

World Council for the Welfare of
the Blind
58, avenue Bosquet, F-75007
Paris, France, (01) 555-6757
(coordinates organizations of and
for the blind by providing
consultation and information)

STATE LISTINGS

The following is a list of ophthalmology departments at medical colleges in the United States that are accredited by the Association of American Medical Colleges.

ALABAMA
Department of Ophthalmology
University of Alabama at
Birmingham
EFH-1
University Station
Birmingham, AL 35294
(205) 934-2014

ARIZONA
Department of Ophthalmology
University of Arizona College of
Medicine
Arizona Health Sciences Center
1501 North Campbell Avenue
Tucson, AZ 85724

ARKANSAS
Department of Ophthalmology
University of Arkansas College of
Medicine
4301 West Markham Street
Slot 523
Little Rock, AR 72205
(501) 661-5150

CALIFORNIA
Department of Ophthalmology
University of Southern California
School of Medicine
2025 Zonal Avenue
Los Angeles, CA 90033
(213) 224-7167

Division of Ophthalmology
Stanford University Medical Center
Stanford, CA 94305
(415) 723-5517

Jules Stein Eye Institute
University of California
800 Westwood Plaza
Los Angeles, CA 90024
(213) 825-6089
(an RP Center that receives support
from the RP Foundation Fighting
Blindness)

COLORADO
Department of Ophthalmology
University of Colorado School of
Medicine
4200 East Ninth Avenue
Denver, CO 80262
(303) 399-1211

CONNECTICUT
Yale Eye Center
Yale University School of Medicine
333 Cedar Street
New Haven, CT 06510
(203) 785-2731

DISTRICT OF COLUMBIA
Department of Ophthalmology
Georgetown University School of
Medicine
3900 Reservoir Road NW
Washington, DC 20007
(202) 625-7121

Department of Ophthalmology
Howard University College of
Medicine
520 West Street NW
Washington, DC 20059
(202) 745-1257

FLORIDA
Bascom-Palmer Eye Institute
University of Medicine
Department of Ophthalmology
900 N.W. 17th Street
Miami, FL 33136
(305) 326-6319
(an RP Center that receives support
from the RP Foundation Fighting
Blindness)
Department of Ophthalmology
University of Florida College of
Medicine
Box J-215, J. Hillis Miller Health
Center
Gainesville, FL 32610
(904) 392-3451

GEORGIA
Emory Eye Center
Emory University School of
Medicine
Atlanta, GA 30322
(404) 321-0111

ILLINOIS
Department of Ophthalmology
Northwestern University Medical
School
303 East Chicago Avenue
Chicago, IL 60611
(312) 908-8649

University of Illinois Eye and Ear
Infirmary
1855 West Taylor Street
Chicago, IL 60612
(312) 996-8938
(an RP Center that receives support
from the RP Foundation Fighting
Blindness)

INDIANA
Department of Ophthalmology
Indiana University Medical Center
702 Rotary Circle
Indianapolis, IN 46202
(317) 274-8937

IOWA
Department of Ophthalmology
University of Iowa College of
Medicine
100 College of Medicine
Administration Building
Iowa City, IA 52242
(319) 353-4843

KANSAS
Department of Ophthalmology
University of Kansas Medical
Center
School of Medicine
39th and Rainbow Boulevard
Kansas City, KS 66103
(913) 588-6600

KENTUCKY
Department of Ophthalmology
University of Kentucky College of
Medicine
800 Rose Street
Lexington, KY 40536
(606) 233-5000

LOUISIANA
Department of Ophthalmology
Tulane University School of
Medicine
1430 Tulane Avenue
New Orleans, LA 70112
(504) 588-5312

MARYLAND
Department of Ophthalmology
Johns Hopkins University School of
Medicine
720 Rutland Avenue
Baltimore, MD 21205
(301) 955-5000

MASSACHUSETTS
Berman-Gund Laboratory for the
Study of Retinal Degenerations
Massachusetts Eye and Ear
Infirmary
Harvard Medical School
243 Charles Street
Boston, MA 02114

(617) 573-3621
(an RP Center that receives support
from the RP Foundation Fighting
Blindness)

Department of Ophthalmology
Tufts University School of Medicine
New England Medical Center
171 Harrison Avenue
Boston, MA 02111
(617) 956-5485

MICHIGAN
Department of Ophthalmology
University of Michigan Medical
Center
W. K. Kellogg Eye Center
1000 Wall Street
Ann Arbor, MI 48105
(313) 763-5874

MINNESOTA
Department of Ophthalmology
Minnesota Medical School
Box 293 UMHC
Minneapolis, MN 55455
(612) 625-4400

MISSISSIPPI
Department of Ophthalmology
University of Mississippi Medical
Center
2500 Jackson, MS 39216
(601) 984-5020

MISSOURI
Department of Ophthalmology
Washington University School of
Medicine
660 South Euclid Avenue
St. Louis, MO 63110
(314) 362-7156

NEBRASKA
Department of Ophthalmology
University of Nebraska College of
Medicine
42nd Street and Dewey Avenue
Omaha, NE 68105
(402) 559-4276

NEW HAMPSHIRE
Department of Ophthalmology
Dartmouth Medical School
Hanover, NH 03756
(603) 646-7505

NEW JERSEY
Department of Medicine and
Dentistry of New Jersey
New Jersey Medical School
150 Bergen Street
Newark, NJ 07103
(201) 456-4300

NEW MEXICO
Department of Ophthalmology
University of New Mexico School of
Medicine
Albuquerque, NM 87131
(505) 277-4151

NEW YORK
College of Physicians and Surgeons
Columbia University
Department of Ophthalmology
630 West 168th Street
New York, NY 10032
(212) 305-5688
(an RP Center that receives support
from the RP Foundation Fighting
Blindness)

Department of Ophthalmology
Cornell University Medical College
1300 York Avenue
New York, NY 10021
(212) 472-5293

New York University Medical
Center
Department of Ophthalmology
530 First Avenue
New York, NY 10016
(212) 340-6435
(an RP Center that receives support
from the RP Foundation Fighting
Blindness)

Department of Ophthalmology
University of Rochester Medical
Center

601 Elmwood Avenue
Rochester, NY 14642
(716) 275-3256

NORTH CAROLINA
Department of Ophthalmology
Duke University Medical Center
Box 3005
Durham, NC 27710
(919) 758-5800

Department of Ophthalmology
University of North Carolina at
  Chapel Hill
School of Medicine
Chapel Hill, NC 27514
(919) 966-5296

NORTH DAKOTA
Department of Ophthalmology
University of North Dakota School
  of Medicine
Grand Forks, ND 58202
(701) 780-6000

OHIO
Department of Ophthalmology
University of Cincinnati Medical
  Center
231 Bethesda Avenue
Cincinnati, OH 45267-0527
(513) 872-5151

OKLAHOMA
Department of Ophthalmology
University of Oklahoma Health
  Sciences Center
P.O. Box 26901
Oklahoma City, OK 73190
(405) 271-4066

OREGON
Department of Ophthalmology
Oregon Health Sciences University
  School of Medicine
3181 S.W. Sam Jackson Park Road
Portland, OR 97201
(503) 225-8311
(503) 225-8386 for RP Center that
  receives support from the RP
  Foundation Fighting Blindness

PENNSYLVANIA
Department of Ophthalmology
Hospital of the University of
  Pennsylvania
3400 Spruce Street
Philadelphia, PA 19104
(215) 662-2762

Department of Ophthalmology
Temple University
School of Medicine
3400 North Broad Street
Philadelphia, PA 19104
(215) 221-4046

SOUTH CAROLINA
Department of Ophthalmology
Medical University of South
  Carolina
171 Ashley Avenue
Charleston, SC 29425
(803) 792-2492

SOUTH DAKOTA
Department of Ophthalmology
University of South Dakota School
  of Medicine
2501 West 22nd Street
Sioux Falls, SD 57105
(605) 665-9638

TENNESSEE
Department of Ophthalmology
Vanderbilt University Medical
  Center
1161 21st Avenue, South
Nashville, TN 37232
(615) 322-2031

TEXAS
Cullen Eye Institute
Baylor College of Medicine
6501 Fannin, Room C109
Houston, TX 77030
(713) 799-5933
(an RP Center that receives support
  from the RP Foundation Fighting
  Blindness)

Department of Ophthalmology
University of Texas Southwestern
   Medical School at Dallas
5323 Harry Hines Boulevard
Dallas, TX 75235
(214) 688-3111

UTAH
Department of Ophthalmology
University of Utah School of
   Medicine
50 North Medical Drive
Salt Lake City, UT 84132
(801) 581-6384

VERMONT
Department of Ophthalmology
University of Vermont College of
   Medicine
Burlington, VT 05405
(802) 656-4516

VIRGINIA
Department of Ophthalmology
University of Virginia School of
   Medicine
Box 395, Medical Center
Charlottesville, VA 22908
(804) 924-0211

WASHINGTON
Department of Ophthalmology
University of Washington School of
   Medicine, RJ-10
Seattle, WA 98195
(206) 543-3883

WEST VIRGINIA
Department of Ophthalmology
Marshall University School of
   Medicine
Huntington, WV 25701
(304) 526-0530

WISCONSIN
Department of Ophthalmology
University of Wisconsin Medical
   School
1300 University Avenue
Madison, WI 53706
(608) 263-4900

CANADIAN LISTINGS

ALBERTA
Department of Ophthalmology
2-129 Clinical Sciences Building
University of Alberta
Edmonton, Alberta T6G 2G3
Canada
(403) 492-6641

MANITOBA
Department of Ophthalmology
GH-604, 820 Sherbrook Street
University of Manitoba
Winnipeg, Manitoba R3A 1R9
Canada
(204) 787-3717

ONTARIO
Department of Ophthalmology
Etherington Hall
Queen's University
Kingston, Ontario K7L 3N6
Canada
(613) 545-2559

Department of Ophthalmology
Toronto Western Hospital
399 Bathurst Street
East Wing, Room 511
Toronto, Ontario M5T 2S8
Canada
(416) 978-2634

QUEBEC
Department of Ophthalmology
Royal Victoria Hospital-McGill
   University
Room 8753
687 Pine Avenue, West
Montreal, Quebec H3A 1A1
Canada
(514) 842-1231

SASKATCHEWAN
Department of Ophthalmology
University of Saskatchewan
c/o University Hospital
Eye Department
Saskatoon, Saskatchewan S7N 0X0
Canada
(306) 966-8045

FURTHER READING

GENERAL

Blakeslee, Alton. "NSPB Scientific Conference." *Sightsaving* 53, no. 3 (1984–85): 18–22.

Chaney, Earlyne. *The Eyes Have It: A Self-help Manual for Better Vision.* York Beach, ME: Weiser, 1987.

Christman, Ernst H. *A Primer on Refraction.* Springfield, IL: Thomas, 1972.

Freese, Arthur S. *The Miracle of Vision.* New York: Harper & Row, 1977.

Hubel, David. *Eye, Brain, and Vision.* San Francisco: Freeman, 1988.

Jampol, Lee, M.D. "Lasers—Past, Present, and Future." *Sightsaving* 53, no. 4 (1984–85): 10–11.

Marr, David. *Vision.* San Francisco: Freeman, 1983.

Silberner, Joane. "Eyeing a Solution." *Science News,* December 15, 1984, 378–79.

Silverstein, Alvin, and Virginia B. Silverstein. *Glasses and Contact Lenses: Your Guide to Eyes, Eyewear, and Eye Care.* New York: Lippincott, 1989.

Simon, Hilda. *Sight and Seeing: A World of Light and Color.* New York: Putnam, 1983.

Weale, R. A. *Focus on Vision.* Cambridge: Harvard University Press, 1983.

White, Lawrence B., and Roy Brockkel. *Optical Illusions.* New York: Watts, 1986.

Zinn, Walter J., and Herbert Solomon. *The Complete Guide to Eye Care, Eyeglasses, and Contact Lenses.* Hollywood, FL: Fell, 1986.

DISORDERS AND DISEASE

Abrahamson, Ira A. *Cataract Surgery.* New York: McGraw-Hill, 1986.

Bartholomew, R. S. *A Practical Guide to Cataract and Lens Implant Surgery.* New York: Churchill, 1987.

Frank, Robert N. "New Hope in Diabetic Retinopathy." *Sightsaving* 53, no. 4 (1984–85).

Glasspool, Michael. *Eyes: Their Problems and Treatments.* New York: Arco, 1984.

Heckenlively, John R., et al. *Retinitis Pigmentosa.* Philadelphia: Lippincott, 1987.

Leychecker, Wolfgang, and Ronald P. Crick. *All About Glaucoma: Questions and Answers for People with Glaucoma.* Winchester, MA: Faber and Faber, 1981.

National Society to Prevent Blindness. "Questions and Answers About Glaucoma." *Sightsaving* 53, no. 1 (1984): 14–20.

Randall, Robert M. "AMD: Age-Related Macular Degeneration." *Sightsaving* 54, no. 1 (1985): 15–19.

Schepens, Charles L. *Retinal Detachment and Allied Diseases.* 2 vols. Philadelphia: Saunders, 1983.

Sigelman, Jesse. *Retinal Diseases: Pathogenesis, Laser Therapy, and Surgery.* Boston: Little, Brown, 1984.

Spencer, William H. *Ophthalmic Pathology: An Atlas and Textbook.* 3 vols. 3rd ed. Philadelphia: Saunders, 1986.

Wilson, Fred M. *So You Have a Retinal Detachment: A Guide for Patients.* Springfield, IL: Thomas, 1978.

BLINDNESS

Ciolino, Nancy, and Jed Horowitz. "What Diabetics Need to Know About Their Risk of Blindness." *Sightsaving* 52, no.1 (1983): 2–5.

Dobree, John H., and Eric Boulter. *Blindness and Visual Handicap: The Facts.* New York: Oxford University Press, 1982.

Tuttle, Dean W. *Self-esteem and Adjusting with Blindness: The Process of Responding to Life's Demands.* Springfield, IL: Thomas, 1984.

Wilson, John. *World Blindness and Its Prevention.* Vol 2. New York: Oxford University Press, 1984.

Wilson, John, and International Agency for the Prevention of Blindness. *World Blindness and Its Prevention.* Vol 1. New York: Oxford University Press, 1980.

GLOSSARY

accommodation the ability of the lens to change shape, enabling the eye to continue focusing as it shifts its view from one distance to another

amblyopia "lazy eye"; the reduction or impairment of vision, especially in one eye; occurs when the brain suppresses the messages of one eye because they are incompatible with those of the other

AMD age-related macular degeneration; a degenerative disease of the macula that usually occurs in people over 55; symptoms include loss of color vision, blurred vision, the appearance of black or gray spots, the perception of vertical lines as wavy ones, and progressive loss of all vision

anterior chamber a space in the eye between the cornea and the front surface of the lens

aqueous humor a clear fluid produced in the eye that flows through the anterior and pituitary chambers and diffuses into the bloodstream

astigmatism a defect of vision caused by an irregularly shaped cornea or lens; this deformity scatters light rays as they enter the eye, forming a blurred image

bifocals bifocal glasses; spectacles comprising two lenses: a smaller lens, located on top, for near vision, and a larger lens, beneath it, for distance vision

binocular vision the use of both eyes together without double vision

blind spot the point in the retina where the optic nerve enters; contains no light-sensitive cells and is therefore unable to perceive images

bullous keratopathy corneal degeneration characterized by great pain and impaired vision; caused by excess fluid buildup that ruptures, exposing corneal nerves

cataract an opaque film that forms and enlarges in the eye, obstructing the passage of light to the eye and impending vision or causing blindness; may be caused by physical injuries to the eye, residual scar tissue, or diseases, such as diabetes, but is most commonly the result of aging

ciliary body a circular structure on the inner surface of the eyeball composed chiefly of the ciliary muscle and tubular folds connected to ligaments

ciliary muscle a muscle, contained in the ciliary body, that contracts and expands to adjust lens shape in visual accommodation

color blindness a colloquial term applied to any deviation from normal perception of hues

cone retinal cell that serves light and color vision; numbering between 6 million and 7 million, cones are found mainly in the macula lutea

conjunctiva the mucous membrane that lines the inner surface of the eyelids and the forepart of the eyeball

conjunctivitis pinkeye; inflammation of the conjunctiva; characterized by one or both eyes being red, swollen, itchy, and discharging pus; caused by exposure to bright light or by a viral or bacterial infection

contact lens a curved shell of glass or plastic applied directly over the cornea to correct refractive errors; "hard" lenses are small and thick and cling loosely to the eye; "soft" lenses are thinner, larger, more flexible, cling closely to the eye, and require moistness

cornea the transparent layer that covers the iris and pupil; the most sensitive part of the eye, the cornea admits light to the interior

depth perception the proper recognition of depth or the relative distances to different objects in space

detached retina separation of the inner layers of the retina from the pigment epithelium (lining); characterized by the appearance of floaters, flashes of light, suddenly blurred vision, and showers of dark spots, or a curtain moving across the eye

deuteranopia a type of dichromasy characterized by inability to detect the color green

diabetic retinopathy vision impairment that occurs when blood vessels leak into the eye, damaging the retina; a common symptom of diabetes

dichromasy dichromatism; partial color blindness; a condition in which one of the three cone pigments is altogether missing, resulting in the inability to distinguish more than two of the three primary light colors

esotropia cross-eye; a form of strabismus in which the focus of the eye notably deviates inward

exotropia walleye; a form of strabismus in which the focus of the eye notably deviates outward

extraocular muscles the six voluntary muscles that move the eyeball

floaters "spots before the eyes"; deposits in the vitreous body that appear as dark spots or wavy lines interfering with normal vision

fovea centralis the depression at the center of the macula lutea; the area of clearest vision, because the retinal layers spread aside at this point, permitting light to fall directly on the cones inside

glaucoma a group of eye diseases characterized by an increase of pressure inside the eye, especially on the retina and optic nerve, generally caused by a buildup of aqueous humor in the front of the eye; progressive sight erosion and blindness result, unless glaucoma is medically treated

hyperopia farsightedness; the condition of minimal refractive power that is characterized by the inability to see near objects clearly

hypertropia a form of strabismus in which the focus of the eye notably deviates upward

hypotropia a form of strabismus in which the focus of the eye notably deviates downward

intraocular implant an implant within the eye; most frequently, the implant of a lens into the eye of a cataract patient whose clouded lens has been removed

iris the colored membrane suspended between the lens and the cornea in the aqueous humor and perforated by the pupil; by contraction and dilation, the iris regulates the amount of light entering the eye

keratoconus conical cornea; a condition characterized by a pointed, protruding cornea that results in myopia; more common in females than in males, and most often develops during puberty

legal blindness blindness as defined by law; 20/200 vision or worse

lens the transparent body of the eye situated between the posterior chamber and the vitreous body; works in conjunction with the cornea to focus light rays entering the eye

melanin the pigment that gives color to the iris, as well as to skin, hair, and other parts of the body

myopia nearsightedness; the condition of increased refractive power that is characterized by the inability to see distant objects clearly

nerve a cordlike structure composed of individual nerve cells that convey, through electrical impulses, information between a part of the central nervous system, such as the brain, and another region of the body, such as the eyes

night blindness nyctalopia; failure or imperfection of vision at night or in dim light, with good vision only in bright light

nodule a small solid bump that sometimes forms on the outer edge of the cornea in the elderly and may impair vision

ophthalmologist oculist; a medical doctor who specializes in examining and treating eyes and is licensed to prescribe medication

optician a person who makes, fits, and sells corrective lenses but does not diagnose eye problems

optometrist doctor of optometry; O.D.; a person specifically trained and licensed to examine the eyes in order to detect vision problems and to prescribe and adapt lenses but who is not a physician and may not prescribe medicine

orbit orbita; the bony cavity that contains the eyeball

photocoagulation the process of condensing protein material by means of an intense beam of light (a laser); used especially in treatment of diabetic retinopathy, retinal tearing, and retinal detachment

posterior chamber a space in the eye between the back of the iris and the lens

presbyopia decreased power of accommodation that occurs in advancing years and is caused by a diminished elasticity of the lens; characterized by hyperopia and generally impaired vision

protanopia a type of dichromasy characterized by inability to detect the color red

pupil the small black opening at the center of the iris through which light enters the eye

refractive power diotropic power; the degree to which the eye bends light rays, determining whether images are focused behind, in front of, or on the retina

retina the sensory membrane lining the posterior chamber of the eye; receives images that have been focused by the lens from light rays collected by the pupil and transmits them to the brain via the optic nerve

retinal vein occlusion RVO; a retinal disorder in which one or more of the connecting veins become blocked, resulting in either an inadequate or excessive supply of blood to the retina; vision impairment may develop into partial or full vision loss if RVO goes untreated

retinitis pigmentosa RP; pigmentary retinopathy; any of several hereditary progressive degenerative eye diseases marked by night blindness in the early stages, retinal atrophy, pigment alteration, and a narrowing of the visual field, potentially leading to blindness

rod retinal cell that serves night vision and motion detection; numbering approximately 12 million, most rods are located on the periphery of the retina

sclera the tough white outer coat of the eyeball

strabismus heterotropia; squint; a condition in which one eyeball, and, accordingly, its field of vision, deviates from the other eye and its focus; usually caused by an imbalance of eyeball muscles

sty hordeolum; an inflammatory infection on the inner or outer edge of the eyelid

tonometer an instrument for measuring tension or pressure; used to detect glaucoma

trachoma a bacterially caused chronic infectious disease of the conjunctiva and cornea; characterized by pain, tearing, swelling, and, if untreated, corneal scarring

trifocals trifocal glasses; spectacles comprising three lenses: the upper for near vision, the middle for intermediate distance vision, and the lower for distance vision

tritanope a form of dichromasy characterized by inability to detect the color blue

vitrectomy surgical removal of the vitreous humor, a thick transparent fluid; used especially in treatment of diabetic retinopathy

vitreous body corpus vitreum; the area between the lens and the retina containing the vitreous humor

xerophthalmia dryness of the conjunctiva and cornea; caused by vitamin A deficiency, xerophthalmia most often affects children in Third World countries

zonules of Zinn zonula ciliaris; a cluster of ligaments that hold the lens in place

INDEX

PICTURE CREDITS

Allergan Pharmaceuticals: pp. 38, 39, 43, 45, 52 (top and bottom), 55, 66, 83; American Academy of Ophthalmology: p. 75; AP/Wide World: pp. 33, 37, 50, 53, 60, 64, 76; Bettmann Archive: pp. 13, 17, 28, 49, 71, 79; Laimute E. Druskis/Taurus: p. 35; Ellen Fiore: p. 52; Charles Marden Fitch/Taurus: p. 19; Bob Hahn/Taurus Photos: p. 69; Eric Kroll/Taurus: pp. 57, 82; Library of Congress: pp. 14, 15; National Library of Medicine: p. 16; L. L. T. Rhodes/ Taurus: p. 26; Martin M. Rotker/Taurus: pp. 30, 31, 32, 63, 72, 74; Jerry Sarapochiello/Bruce Coleman: cover; UPI/Bettmann Newsphotos: p. 68; Original illustrations by Nisa Rauschenberg: pp. 20, 21, 23, 25, 41, 81

Jane Samz, a science writer and editor, graduated from Smith College and received an M.A. in history of science from the University of Wisconsin. She is the author of science articles for encyclopedia yearbooks, the coauthor of *Voyage to Jupiter* for NASA, and the author of *Drugs and Diet* in the Chelsea House ENCYCLOPEDIA OF PSYCHOACTIVE DRUGS.

Dale C. Garell, M.D., is medical director of California Children Services, Department of Health Services, County of Los Angeles. He is also associate dean for curriculum at the University of Southern California School of Medicine and clinical professor in the Department of Pediatrics & Family Medicine at the University of Southern California School of Medicine. From 1963 to 1974, he was medical director of the Division of Adolescent Medicine at Children's Hospital in Los Angeles. Dr. Garell has served as president of the Society for Adolescent Medicine, chairman of the youth committee of the American Academy of Pediatrics, and as a forum member of the White House Conference on Children (1970) and White House Conference on Youth (1971). He has also been a member of the editorial board of the *American Journal of Diseases of Children.*

C. Everett Koop, M.D., Sc.D., is former Surgeon General, Deputy Assistant Secretary for Health, and Director of the Office of International Health of the U.S. Public Health Service. A pediatric surgeon with an international reputation, he was previously surgeon-in-chief of Children's Hospital of Philadelphia and professor of pediatric surgery and pediatrics at the University of Pennsylvania. Dr. Koop is the author of more than 175 articles and books on the practice of medicine. He has served as surgery editor of the *Journal of Clinical Pediatrics* and editor-in-chief of the *Journal of Pediatric Surgery,* Dr. Koop has received nine honorary degrees and numerous other awards, including the Denis Brown Gold Medal of the British Association of Paediatric Surgeons, the William E. Ladd Gold Medal of the American Academy of Pediatrics, and the Copernicus Medal of the Surgical Society of Poland. He is a Chevalier of the French Legion of Honor and a member of the Royal College of Surgeons, London.